Bio Richthofen von

10-2300

Quality

10/09

D0931928

THE RED BARON

THE RED BARON

by

MANRED VON RICHTOFEN

Pen & Sword
AVIATION

WEST BRIDGEWATER PUBLIC LIBRARY
80 HOWARD ST.
WEST BRIDGEWATER, MA 02379

First published in Great Britain in 1994 by Leo Cooper

Republished in this format in 2009 by
Pen & Sword Military
An imprint of
Pen & Sword Books Ltd
47 Church Street
Barnsley
South Yorkshire
S70 2AS

Copyright © Manfred Von Richtofen, 2009

ISBN 978 184415 886 7

The right of Ray Westlake to be identified as Author of this work has
been asserted by him in accordance with the Copyright, Designs and
Patents Act 1988.

A CIP catalogue record for this book is
available from the British Library

All rights reserved. No part of this book may be reproduced or
transmitted in any form or by any means, electronic or mechanical
including photocopying, recording or by any information storage and
retrieval system, without permission from the
Publisher in writing.

Printed and bound in England
By CPI

Pen & Sword Books Ltd incorporates the Imprints of Pen & Sword
Aviation,
Pen & Sword Family History, Pen & Sword Maritime, Pen & Sword
Military, Wharncliffe Local History,
Pen & Sword Select, Pen & Sword Military Classics, Leo Cooper,
Remember When, Seaforth Publishing and Frontline Publishing

For a complete list of Pen & Sword titles please contact
PEN & SWORD BOOKS LIMITED
47 Church Street, Barnsley, South Yorkshire, S70 2AS, England
E-mail: enquiries@pen-and-sword.co.uk
Website: www.pen-and-sword.co.uk

CONTENTS

ILLUSTRATIONS

1. Manfred von Richthofen. (NH)
2. Oswald Boelcke, seated in a Jasta 2 Albatros DI, late 1916. (CB)
3. Von Richthofen, Spring 1917. (CB)
4. Oswald Boelcke prior to his award of Pour Le Mérite. (NH)
5. Albatros DII flown by Leutnant Max Böhme. (CB)
6. Von Richthofen seated in the cockpit of his Albatros Scout, 1917. (CB)
7. Leutnant Kurt Wolff and von Richthofen in Belgium. (NH)
8. Line up of Jasta 11 on Douai airfield in April 1917. (NH)
9. General Ludendorff inspecting Jasta 11 at Marcke, Belgium, August 1917. (CB)
10. Von Richthofen and Wilhelm Reinhard. (NH)
11. Oblt Eduard Dostler upon his award in August 1917 of the Pour Le Mérite. (NH)
12. Von Richthofen with his Pour Le Mérite, Iron Cross 1st and 2nd class and pilot's badge. (NH)
13. Von Richthofen, the Red Air Fighter. (NH)

PUBLISHER'S NOTE

The footnotes to the text of *The Red Air Fighter* are those written for the first English edition by C.G. Grey, the editor of *The Aeroplane*. Notes based on current historical research will be found at the end of this book, together with comprehensive information on Manfred von Richthofen's victories and the aeroplanes that he flew.

The Publishers are grateful to Mr. Norman Franks and to Mr. N.H. Hauprich for their help in providing the above information, and to Mr. Hauprich and to Mr. Chaz Bowyer for the photographs included with this new edition.

1990

INTRODUCTION

by Norman Franks

IT HAS been over 70 years since Manfred von Richthofen's original *The Red Air Fighter* (*Der Rote Kampfflieger*) was published in Germany in 1917, the year before he was killed in action over the Somme battlefields in France.

Although the war was still being fought in France, such was the interest in von Richthofen that the book was immediately translated into English and in 1918 published in both England and the United States of America.

Since then much has been written about the famed Red Baron, and of his Flying Circus, Jagdgeschwader Nr.1. There can be little doubt that von Richthofen was one of the best fighter pilots the Germans had in World War One, not just because he was credited with the most aerial victories of any of the warring nations but because he was the master of his trade – a trade that he, and all other air fighters of that war, had had to learn for themselves. There were no pilot's notes or approved tactics memoranda to study. The only guidance he and others had in 1916 was from his commander in Jasta 2, the famous Oswald Boelcke, who had himself been self-taught.

Another sign of Richthofen's greatness is that he, too, was able to show his own junior pilots how it was done; he was a natural leader and held in high esteem by his superiors.

Not all of the many stories, books and articles about him have put von Richthofen in a good light; some, indeed have been quite disparaging. But, if the last 70 years have taught us anything, it is to look at the First World War in a more positive way, as one looks at earlier wars and the men who fought them.

It is often the case that those who write of such men as von Richthofen are on the victorious side – the winners. It is they who more often than not try to dictate how future generations should view a conflict or a person in that conflict. So it was with von Richthofen. The years in which the story of the First Great War in the Air could be told, the 1930s, became the heyday of both the pulp-writers, and of those who tried earnestly to be objective about the recent Great War; in those years the aviation market was flooded with stories of battles fought above the Western Front. Some were good, some fanciful, some even totally untrue or at best, over-romantic. There were plenty of heroes among the winners, whether alive or dead.

When it came to the "enemy", however, there were those who tried to be objective, others condescending, while a few felt the need to be totally against any idea that any German airman had been good. Naturally, the majority of these latter writers had not fought in the war, certainly not been in the airforce. Thus some of the tales about the German "aces" began to be distorted for the general public, who were now clamouring to hear about that world above the trenches, the mighty gash of earthworks that ran from the Channel coast to the border with Switzerland, where the Knights of the Air fought duels with their chivalrous adversaries.

Manfred von Richthofen, being the greatest of the

German fighting pilots – he had to be, he had shot down the most! – was a natural target for the sensation writers. Most of his victories were obsolete two-seaters, they wrote; he always fought with his squadrons protecting his back; he claimed many victories that his men had shot down; he always tried to surprise his victims, shooting them down without giving them a chance – and so it went on. The truth is a little less sensational.

Let us examine some of these statements: obsolete two-seaters. As the RFC and RAF were using aeroplanes in front line service, the term "obsolete" isn't really correct. The fact that some of these aircraft were inferior in performance, both in speed, firepower and manoeuvrability, doesn't make them obsolete. And if they were flying an inferior machine, whose fault was that? Certainly it wasn't Manfred von Richthofen's.

Being a dedicated soldier for his country, it was his job to attack and shoot down his country's enemies. There could be no question of his not attacking because he was in a better aeroplane! Those same two-seaters were often helping to guide Allied shell-fire down onto German positions, German troops, his fellow countrymen. Of course he had to help stop that happening. That the BE2Cs or RE8s of the British Corps squadrons were slower was part and parcel of their job; one couldn't direct gunfire or make a detailed reconnaissance in a fast aeroplane! Most of the time, these Corps aircraft were protected by single-seater patrols, but it didn't always work out that way. Life is never that easy.

The assertions that von Richthofen flew with his men protecting him, or that he claimed victories that others had scored are correct on the one hand, but totally wrong on the other. The German fighting squadrons, the Jastas, were hunting units, designed specifically to seek out the enemy aeroplanes and stop them doing their work, whether it be directing gunfire, taking photographs of the German positions, observing what the Germans were doing behind their front lines, bombing them, attacking the trenches, or protecting other machines. Like hunters, they flew in packs, ready to bring the maximum of their number into a battle situation, in order to do the maximum damage.

When the Jastas were formed in the summer of 1916, they consisted of 12 pilots and aeroplanes, with a Jasta commander. These 12 were generally divided into two subsections and the commander would usually alternate as leader of each sub-section, sometimes of five aeroplanes, but usually of six. Thus one man of each section could have a day off, or a man might have reported sick, etc. In 1916, these six men would fly patrols to the front lines, but stay well back from them, and seek out any French or British aeroplanes, working above the trenches. Often they would not even take to the air until front-line troops reported British or French machines actually in the act of crossing the front lines. Depending on where these intruders were, they could even be seen from the Jasta airfields, and powerful field glasses were generally on hand to view them prior to take-off!

The good and able commanders would not generally rush into the battle with guns blazing, but rather size up the situation, fly until they were in the most favourable position to make a successful attack, and then dive upon their opponents. If the opposition comprised just one lone machine, then the commander would generally be the first to have the opportunity to bring that aeroplane down, safe in the knowledge that his men were keeping a watch for other hostile aeroplanes, while he concentrated on the job in hand. If there were two enemy aircraft, the next senior pilot might take on the second machine, and only if there was a larger formation of, say, bombing aircraft engaged, would the six Jasta pilots split up and fight individually, after the initial attacking swoop.

Far from being something to deride, these tactics were simply the most efficient way of maximising one's forces in order to inflict the maximum hurt upon one's foe. It was a good theory put into even better practice. The German Jasta pilots became adept at this method of air warfare – the list of RFC casualties in 1917 alone stands testimony to that.

Throughout the First War, the Allied airmen were indoctrinated into taking the war to the enemy. Theirs was always an offensive war. Daily the Royal Flying Corps, and later the RAF headquarters, sent out men and machines to make reconnaissance flights, both short and long, photographic sorties, bombing raids, and so on. They chose two methods of protection. One was some form of close escort by fighting aeroplanes, the other was offensive patrols in the general area of the other machines, in order to engage would-be attackers. These offensive patrols, OPs, would also provide opportunity to attack any German two-seaters they spotted doing similar work to their own Corps aircraft, who might similarly be protected by single-seaters. In this way, some of the air battles, known later as dog-fights, began.

Both sides had strict rules covering the claim of pilots to have downed an opponent in air combat. As the vast majority of the battles were fought over the German side of the lines, it followed that claims by German pilots were easier to verify. The wreckage could be viewed, bodies found or prisoners taken. From the very early days of air fighting, there was a certain kudos in bringing down an opponent. In early 1915 it was fast becoming a common occurrence but nevertheless an important "victory" for the pilot. By the middle of that year, when the first single-seater Fokker monoplanes began to be attached to German two-seater units for protection purposes, the rise to fame of a few of the early pioneers of air fighting began. Immelmann, Boelcke, Wintgens, von Multzer, Parschau – all became famous in these early days. Boelcke eventually became known as the father of German fighting tactics, and it was he, in 1916, who saw the potential in a two-seater pilot on the Russian front – Manfred von Richthofen.

The rule that applied to victories on the German side was that the enemy aeroplane had to be located, either intact or wreckage, at the place the pilot said he brought it down, and verified either by other men in the air or by ground observers. Any that fell or landed on the Allied side of the trenches were often not confirmed, unless someone else actually saw it crash beyond reasonable repair, burn, or it was shelled subsequently by gunfire and seen to be destroyed. This system did not leave much room for a pilot to try to increase his own score either by deception or by taking another's claim. Anyone who tried and was caught out, soon left the front line squadron!

On the British side, confirming victories was more difficult, but as long as the aeroplane attacked was seen to crash, burn or in some other way be destroyed, and verified again by either air or ground observers, it was credited to the victorious pilot. However, with the difficulty of flying above cloud or very high up, perhaps hotly engaged by other aircraft, it was not always possible to observe the fate of an aircraft that appeared to be going down for the last time – generally in a spinning nose dive or even an all-out plunge earthwards. This gave rise to the term ''Out of Control'' as a claim – what in World War Two was known as a probable kill. Pilots of both sides, of course, used this spinning down manoeuvre as a ruse to get out of trouble, and when near the ground would regain proper control and fly off. But provided another pilot saw and confirmed what he thought was a machine going down "out of control" and looking certain to crash, this "probable" victory was confirmed and listed as a victory. This happened throughout the war, even though in the second half of 1918, the number of "OOC" claims had so increased owing to the intensity of the air fighting, that only crashed or flaming victories were listed in the RAF Communiqués.

The RFC also had a category in the early days of Forced to Land (FTL). This was when a pilot shot at a German aircraft, which went down and landed – on its own side of the front of course. Again this was a good way of getting out of trouble – unless the British pilot took it into his head to follow the machine down and shoot it up on the ground (chivalry often checked a pilot's urge to do this – but not always!). Yet by the same token, the pilot might have been seriously or even mortally wounded, or his aeroplane so disabled it was effectively destroyed, even though the pilot's skill had enabled him to land it. So this could be argued to be another form of "probable" victory and was credited. In any event, the German machine and its pilot had certainly been stopped doing the work it was engaged upon over the front. This form of victory was added to a pilot's score (despite later historians' views to the contrary) till late in 1916, after which the aircraft forced to land had to be seen to be completely out of action. In the later stages of the war, chivalry was less obvious and the Allied pilot, if given the chance, would shoot up the aeroplane and crew on the ground!

Finally, the charge that von Richthofen often surprised his victims and gave them no chance to defend themselves. Very commendable – that was precisely his job. The fighter pilot – they were called scout pilots in WW1 – is trained to do exactly that; to destroy the maximum enemy forces with the minimum risk to himself and his fellow pilots. By his very trade he has to gain the advantage of position and strike to advantage. Why risk a dog-fight in which the opponent may kill you when you can kill him without being seen? It may not sound chivalrous – a term somewhat over-used when describing WW1 air warfare – but it got the job done!

One final item that should be kept in mind about the tactics and conditions of flying on the Western Front, is the prevailing wind, which is from the south-west. This gave the German scout pilots the advantage, for as British fuel tanks began to dry, the pilots had to fly back home in the face of any wind that might be blowing, and in a fight, the battle would inevitably start to drift east – further and further into enemy territory. Little wonder the Germans let the enemy flyers come to them, for they could choose the moment of battle and hold the ace card – the weather. Little wonder, too, that wherever possible, the German scouts would endeavour to place themselves between the lines and their opponents, so that they would have to fly past them to get to safety.

Manfred von Richthofen was in his early twenties when he was at the height of his fame as a national hero and success-ful fighting pilot. When he fell in combat he was just a matter of days away from his 26th birthday. By that time he had been fighting for his country for three and a half years, firstly as a cavalry officer, then a flying observer and finally as a pilot.

As a pilot, he, along with many others, had been reading the almost daily exploits of such men as Max Immelmann and Oswald Boelcke on the Western Front, bringing down French and British machines and gaining high honours and rewards. Little wonder that many desired to follow such paths to glory. Von Richthofen had his chance when the great Boelcke, victor in 19 aerial fights during 1915–16, was taken away from the war front and told to form fighting units of fighting single-seater machines. The practice of having one or two "scouts" with each two-seater Staffel was ending. In future, the scouts would be formed into separate fighting units.

Thus by mid-1916, with his help, the first seven Jastas were being formed with eight more by August, 33 by the end of the year. Each Jasta was smaller in size than an RFC squadron, although by the end of 1917, the establishment had risen from a dozen pilots, to eighteen. Boelcke himself was forbidden to fly in action, being deemed too important to be put at risk, so he was sent off on a tour of the south-eastern front.

While he was thus engaged, the Battle of the Somme opened on the Western Front. Immelmann had fallen shortly beforehand, so Boelcke was recalled and ordered to head one of the new Jastas, Jasta 2. He was able to recruit his own pilots, one of whom was Manfred von Richthofen whom he had met while on the Eastern Front.

Von Richthofen's transition to single-seater scouting aircraft was fairly swift, but it was Boelcke who opened the Jasta's scoring, bringing down seven English aeroplanes in the first two weeks of September 1916. But then the Jasta was still awaiting its aircraft; Boelcke was flying one of two Fokker DIIIs that had arrived and which, with one Albatros DI, was all they had. On the 16th some Albatros DIIs arrived, and on this day Leutnant Walter Hohne brought down the Jasta's eighth victory.

Boelcke's pilots had watched in awe and impatience as he added to his score, while they could only sit and wait for the opportunity to fly against the enemy flyers. Finally on 17th September, with sufficient aeroplanes to fly a small patrol, Boelcke deemed his "chicks" ready for the test of front line combat. It was a Sunday, but war has no days of the week, or weekends. Jasta 2 found a formation of BE2Cs of 12 Squadron, escorted by FE2bs of 11 Squadron, heading for Marcoing railway station. Climbing above the RFC machines, Boelcke finally attacked and in the ensuing battle, four FE2bs were shot down, three by Boelcke, Hans Reimann and von Richthofen, while Leutnant Erwin Bohme brought down a Sopwith 1½ Strutter of 70 Squadron on this day. Boelcke had his 27th victory, von Richthofen his first!

Until his death in an unfortunate collision during an air battle on 28th October, Boelcke led his Jasta well, bringing his own total air victories to 40 and the Jasta's to 51. By then Richthofen himself had been credited with six. Boelcke's loss was grievous to both Germany and his Jasta 2, but his men carried on in his name and by the end of 1916, they had achieved 86 victories.

It was now that the legend of Baron Manfred von Richthofen was born. In every respect he was just another squadron pilot, but with the good fortune to bring down the occasional British machine. His score rose to ten on 20th November with double victories but on the 23rd he shot down a DH2 single-seater scout, whose pilot was the hero of the British – Major Lanoe Hawker VC DSO, commander of 24 Squadron.

Those who would seek to denigrate von Richthofen's ability as a pilot often choose to forget that for every inferior machine he brought down he also brought down one which was in many respects a match for his own, and occasionally a pilot who was also his equal. On this occasion, the fight between von Richthofen and Hawker lasted for over half an hour, without either man achieving an advantage, so their flying skill must have been of equal standing. As von

Richthofen found, his Albatros could climb faster but Hawker's DH2 turned better.

Finally it was the wind that helped von Richthofen overcome Hawker. With his petrol running low Hawker had to eventually make a dash for the lines or come down and be taken prisoner. He tried it several times but von Richthofen was always ready for him, forcing him to turn again or be shot. Eventually a dash to the lines again caught out the British pilot and a burst from von Richthofen's Albatros Scout hit Hawker in the head. Von Richthofen had his eleventh, and perhaps his most important victory. He was soon a household name, the hero he had wanted to become.

No sooner had he established himself amongst the successful air fighters of the German Air Service, than he was given command of his own squadron, Jasta 11. After leading that, he was given command of a group of four squadrons, Jastas 4, 6, 10, and 11. This was his ''Flying Circus'' – JG Nr1.

Von Richthofen's eventual 80 aerial victories, credited to him during some ten months of front line war flying, must stand as a testament to his ability as a hunting pilot. *The Red Air Fighter* of course only covers the period of his first 52 victories, but if we look at his 80, we can see that a large number were aircraft which could have matched his in performance, especially with the right pilot. A good number of his victims must by the law of averages have been inexperienced in comparison to himself, but then others, like Hawker for instance, had equal experience and expertise. At least one of his victims had been in France for less than a week, but again, that was the system, it was not von Richthofen's fault. The Germans too sent men of limited training to the front when the need was great.

If we take the number of BEs, RE8s, 1½ Strutters, the Morane, the Martinsyde, even the FE8, Pups and the DH5 as being inferior, that accounts for 36. Even here one could argue that a Sopwith Pup or a DH5 in the right hands could beat an Albatros – and did so quite often. And one must bear in mind that the quality of the pilot is all important. By the same token, the FE2b aeroplane was formidable in good hands and when flown in the most advantageous formation. One FE2b squadron held a record for enemy machines shot down at one stage of the war. Von Richthofen claimed 13 FE2bs – and another got him!

And what of the machines that were equal to his in the air battles? Sopwith Camels, SE5s, Spads, Nieuports, Bristol Fighters, the Dolphin, as well as possibly the DH2 (there were a number of DH2 aces)? These account for 31! Of these scouting types, there were a few experienced pilots flying them, who had their own limited share of successes in air fighting. Hawker, of course, had nine victories of the period. A month later Richthofen shot down Gerald Knight, recently awarded the DSO, for having shot down at least five German machines. John Hay of 40 Squadron, shot down in January, had three kills, Captain Barwell of the same squadron (29th April 1917) was credited with six – and that fight lasted another half an hour. Captains Kirkham and Hedley of 20 Squadron had about a dozen victories between them as pilot and gunner. Captain S.P. Smith of 46 Squadron was a daring and press-on type of air fighter and had 10 victories; even von Richthofen's 79th victim, Major Raymond-Barker, had achieved 7 victories. So there were several air fighters who had more than a chance against von Richthofen, but fell to his guns, and it must be said too, his flying skill.

His skill as a pilot must be unquestioned. Men of limited ability didn't last long on the Western Front without being able to stay alive in an air battle. That he could combine that skill with the ability to shoot straight and well – something that doesn't come just because one can fly – made him deadly in the air. He had also learned the lessons of his tutor and mentor, Oswald Boelcke, to position himself for the best place to attack; to choose his battle ground, and, as his combat reports show, he often let the British pilot make the first move, so that he was then able to engage or break off the action, depending on whether the other man had achieved, or might achieve, a more favourable position. It is also, perhaps, significant, that Richthofen never attacked Allied observation balloons, a most dangerous target, being usually well protected by guns and scout patrols!

This is what made von Richthofen a great war pilot, remaining cool and steady in a combat situation, not go all-or-nothing, like so many of his adversaries tried to do. There is a phrase in WW1 parlance, often seen in citations for decorations, showing "dash and courage". Dash and courage is all very well, and it may achieve a limited objective; in the air it may gain a victory or two, but often ended in a swift death. All very commendable and it helped the hero image, but how much better to stay cool, calm and thus achieve 80 victories! But the British and German pilots often fought a different kind of air war. Indeed, the very nature of the British and German fighting man is different.

Von Richthofen must have made a few mistakes – he was human after all – but in the air we remember only two. On 6th July 1917, in a running fight with FE2b aircraft of 20 Squadron, he chased one for just that bit too long and allowed the gunner, Second Lieutenant A.E. Woodbridge, to get in a burst, a bullet from which struck von Richthofen a glancing blow to the head. Woodbridge and his pilot, Captain D.C. Cunnell, were again experienced airmen who had both scored victories in air fights. Von Richthofen managed to land safely, but he had been lucky.

His second mistake was in chasing Second Lieutenant

INTRODUCTION

W.R. May (209 Squadron) for too long, but more than this, he allowed himself to take that pursuit over the front line trenches at low level and thus be subjected to ground fire, something he should never have allowed to happen. In this position he was prey to an attack from behind by another Camel pilot, Captain Roy Brown of the same squadron, as well as from ground fire from Australian soldiers manning that section of the front. This occurred on 21st April 1918, over the Somme valley, in what was to be von Richthofen's last fight.

Hit by a single bullet, the Red Air Fighter, in his all red Fokker triplane, made a rough landing by the Bray-Corbie road, on the Allied side of the lines. The pilot didn't get out – he was dead.

PREFACE

to the First Edition
by C.G. Grey

SOME time ago a Naval Officer who was engaged on particularly hazardous duty was discussing calmly the chances that he and his like had of surviving the war, assuming that it continued for several more years and that his particular branch of it increased its intensity. He wound up his remarks by saying, "The chief reason why I particularly want to survive the finish is that I'm so keen on comparing notes with our opposite numbers in the German Navy."

That is the answer to those who ask, as an important official gentleman asked recently, why this English translation of Manfred von Richthofen's book should be published. It gives our flying people an opportunity of comparing notes with one of Germany's star-turn fighting pilots, just as that excellent book, "An Airman's Outings," by "Contact," gives the Germans the chance of knowing the Royal Flying Corps as it was in 1916 and 1917.

"The Red Air-Fighter" has evidently been carefully censored by the German authorities. Also it has obviously been touched up here and there for propagandist purposes. Consequently, although the narrative as it stands is extraordinarily interesting, the book as a whole is still more interesting on account of what one reads between the lines, and of what one can deduce from the general outlook of the writer. There is, perhaps, little to learn of immediate topical interest, but there is much that explains things which were rather difficult to understand in the past, and the understanding of such points gives one a line of reasoning which should be useful to our active-service aviators in the future.

When one makes due allowance for the propagandist nature of the book, which gives one the general impression of the writings of a gentleman prepared for publication by a hack journalist, one forms a distinctly favourable mental picture of the young Rittmeister Manfred Freiherr von Richthofen.

Our old friend Froissart is credited with the statement that in his age it was always "impossible to inculcate into the German knights the true spirit of knightliness." Which seems to indicate that the practical German mind of those days could not understand the whimsicalities of the Latin ideas of chivalry, which – for example – bade a knight against whose shield an opponent "brake his spear" haul off out of the fight till the lance-less enemy unsheathed his sword and "drave into the combat" again. Probably the Hun of the period proceeded to stick his opponent in the midriff – wherever it may be – and so finished the fight.

In the same true spirit of knightliness an Englishman knocks a man down and then stands back so that he can get up and have another chance, whereas a more practical person would take excellent care that his opponent never got up till he had acknowledged himself beaten. It is all a matter of the point of view, and largely no doubt a matter of education. However, making due allowance for the point of view, one finds surprisingly little Hunnishness in von Richthofen's manners or methods as set forth in print.

It is one of the accepted facts of the war that the German

aviators have displayed greater chivalry than any other branch of the German services. It was a common occurrence for their pilots to fly over our lines in the course of their business, and, by way of variety from that business, to drop packets containing letters from captured British aviators or the personal belongings of the dead. One gathers that these acts of courtesy have become less frequent of late, owing to the intensification of aerial warfare, but it seems that captured and killed aviators still receive the full courtesies of war from the German aviators, whatever may be the fate of prisoners in other hands afterwards.

It is not surprising therefore to find that, taking him all round, Rittmeister von Richthofen conveys to one the general impression that, *mutatis mutandis*, he is very like an English public school boy of good family. His egotism, as one finds it in the book, is the egotism of a young man who is frankly pleased with himself, but is more elated by his good luck than by his cleverness.

In so far as he adopts a superior attitude towards all his enemies he is much less offensive than the superior attitude of the Englishman of the period which produced the couplet:-

"Two skinny Frenchmen, one Portuguee,
One jolly Englishman lick 'em all three."

Happily that type of Englishman has been dead for some years, and his descendants have lost much of his point of view by contact with our gallant Allies of to-day, but he was a common type in his time, even among those commonly known in that period as "the gentry." Who then can blame one of the Teuton race, which by reason of its being so many degrees further East is just so many degrees further removed from the current idea of knightliness, for not possessing precisely the humility which is the pride of good form in these days?

In his own account of his birth and education we find that von Richthofen fulfils all the requirements for the making of a first-class pilot. His people were not politicians, nor even professional soldiers; they were horsemen and game-shots. He was never good at "learning things," and thought it foolish at school "to do more than was just sufficient to pass." But he took prizes for gymnastics. All of which is very like the son of an English country gentleman, if one reads "doing well at footer and cricket" instead of "prizes for gymnastics."

Healthy German discipline is shown in the fact that he went into the Army because his father wished it, and not because he wanted to do so. But that again is only the old patriarchal English system, now, alas, falling, one fears, into a state of nocuous desuetude. On this showing the young von Richthofen could not help making a good pilot any more than any healthy descendant of our own sporting squirearchy can help flying well.

Taking him by and large one rather likes von Richthofen, and one fancies that most of the R.F.C. people who have fought him would have been pleased after the war to sit at table with him and compare notes over the cigarettes and liqueurs, as my Naval friend wants to do with his pre-war friends of the German Navy. And there are unhappily not too many of our present enemies of whom one would like to express such an opinion.

When one comes to read into the book one begins to find many interesting things about the German Army, and the war in general, as well as about the German Feldfliegertruppen – or Flying Service. The German is not really a skilful censor. Just as certain portraits painted by an artist at Ruhleben conveyed by the expression of the faces a good deal that Germany would like hidden, so von Richthofen's book, though carefully censored, lets out quite a good deal of information.

The first thing that strikes one is that Germany's standing army at the beginning of the war was nothing like so perfect a fighting machine as we in this country believed. Although, like all the people with any sense in this country, the German Army knew that a war was coming, the officers and men seem to have set about their work in a singularly amateurish way, judging by the short section of the book devoted to the opening of the war on the Russian Front. And one is pleased to find that von Richthofen had the grace to laugh at himself and his brother-officers for their mistakes.

The episode of the hysterical outburst of his Uhlans when somebody let off a rifle in a tunnel on their way to the West Front discloses a side of German character very unlike the stolid machine-made German to which our publicists have accustomed us. Those who have been long connected with aeronautics may recollect that when Berlin went wild over the looping-the-loop exhibitions of little M. Pégoud, the able German correspondent of "The Aeroplane," Miss Stella Bloch, in recounting the behaviour of the crowd at Johannisthal, described Berlin as the most hysterical capital in Europe. Evidently the mob psychology of the German is a thing which has not been studied by our national leaders, and such incidents as these give one to think furiously as to what may happen if and when the iron military discipline of Germany breaks, and as to what might be done to affect German nerves by a skilfully organised enemy of that country.

A little later in the book one is struck by the singularly unsoldierly way in which the German cavalry patrol work was done. Even the most careless and cocksure British officer of the type which was fairly well eliminated from the British Army by the South African war could not have run blindly into an ambush with greater success, nor could he have got out of it with less military precision.

Also it is consoling to learn that the German troops were as cheerfully ignorant of the fact that the black Maltese Cross on the wings of an aeroplane indicated it to be German as our own and the French troops were that the circles on the wings indicated the aircraft of the Allies; and that the Germans fired on all aeroplanes, irrespective of markings, with the same delightful impartiality as did the Allies' soldiers.

All these things help one to understand why the Germans did not reach Paris with their first thrust, nor Calais with their second. Also they confirm one's belief that, for all Germany's years of militarism, the original British Expeditionary Force was in every way the finest army the world has seen since the legions of Julius Caesar conquered the contemporary world. And the more one realises that fact the greater seems the crime of those who denied to this country before the war the blessing of a big standing army and the boon of compulsory military service.

In some ways the soldiers of all nations resemble one another strongly. For instance, one finds in this book the same contempt for what the Germans picturesquely call a ''base-hog,'' as the French have for the ''embusqué'' and as the British front-line officer has for the young and able-bodied officer who is ''Something on the Staff.'' This is the same in all armies, and they must be clearly distinguished from the carefully trained and expensively educated General Staff Officer, who is very much of a specialist and is the very brain of the Army.

When we come to the purely aviatic portion of the book one finds more of the real von Richthofen and less of the

cavalry officer. His honesty about his utter mental confusion the first time he went into the air recalls General
Brancker's famous remark in his lecture to the Aeronautical
Society when he said that none ever sees anything at all
during his first hour in the air owing to the hopeless confusion in his mind caused by the novel aspect of everything.
Von Richthofen's description of his experience is about the
best thing that has been written on the subject.

An interesting bit of information is disclosed in his
description of his flight in a ''Grossflugzeug,'' on September 1st, 1915. At that period little was known about twin-
engined aeroplanes. The Germans were known to have
tried them, but they were not a success. The only example
known to our people – though probably there were actually
several different machines – was commonly known in the
R.F.C as ''Wong-wong,'' on account of the curious noise
made by the engines or air-screws when they got ''out of
phase'' – as an electrician might call it. This noise is now
quite familiar to the inhabitants of South-Eastern England
as the characteristic note of the Gotha bombers.

Von Richthofen's good judgment of fighting values,
though he was then only an observer, and a novice at that, is
shown by his disapproval of the twin-engined aeroplane as a
fighting machine. It is also of interest to learn that at that
period the Germans had tried an auto-lock device to hold
the rudder of a twin-engined machine over to one side so
that it would fly straight if one engine went out of action,
an ingenious idea even if foredoomed to failure.

It is encouraging to find that though these twin-engined
machines were in operation in September, 1915, the first
bombing squadron so composed only came into action
against defenceless Bucharest a year later. This shows that
actually we in this country are not so very much slower
in producing our new ideas, for our big Handley Page

31

twin-engined biplanes first flew towards the end of 1915, and we began to use them regularly early in 1917 – only a little more than a year later.

The similarity of aviators in all countries is shown by von Richthofen's frank confession of blue funk when he made his first flight alone. That first solo is always the most anxious time in a pilot's career. Another touch of that nature which makes all aviators akin is seen in his accounts of how he and other pupils under instruction used to fly off on cross-country training trips and suffer from opportune forced landings in the parks of their friends or in likely-looking estates. One imagined that this manifestation of "wangling" was an essentially English trick, and would not have been tolerated for a moment under the iron discipline of the German Army. In the early days of the R.F.C. this looking for opulent hosts used to be known sarcastically as "hunting for Jew-palaces."

Seeing the worldwide reputation won by von Richthofen, it is of interest to note that his first appearance as an active service pilot was not until the end of April, 1916, so that at the time of his death, on April 21st – when it was officially stated that von Richthofen had brought down 80 victims – it is really only two years since he first appeared as a war-pilot. Doubtless there are British pilots with as fine a record, or even finer; also it must be remembered that the Germans count kite-balloons among their scores; but even so there is no denying that von Richthofen was a very remarkable young man.

The state of affairs on the Russian front is well shown in the brief reference in the book. "Flying in the East is absolutely a holiday," says the writer, who adds that there was no danger on the Russian front, except the danger of being massacred by the Russians if brought down by engine failure. From which one understands that the Russians did not approve of making prisoners of enemy aviators. Their "Archies" were apparently good, but too few to be useful, and their aviators practically did not exist. Which is rather what one ventured to surmise in print at the time, despite the magniloquent Russian communiqués. When one thinks of all the good British and French aeroplanes and engines which were sent to Russia one regrets the waste of material.

On the subject of air fighting, von Richthofen is always worth studying carefully. None will dispute his wisdom in laying stress on the importance of calmness in an air fight. We have lost many good fighting pilots through their getting excited and dashing headlong into an unequal combat. He, or his editor, has been sufficiently skilful not to give away his pet method of attack. However, one gathers that he depended largely on his first rush for his results, rather than on a prolonged series of manœuvres, except in a single-handed fight with one opponent.

His dictum that "in air fighting results depend on ability and not on trickery," rather bears out this impression. Nevertheless he occasionally tells of a lengthy tussle with a particularly skilful enemy.

Such a story relates how that very gallant gentleman, Major Lanoe Hawker, one of the best loved and admired of the R.F.C's many gallant fighting leaders, fell. It is known that Major Hawker's machine was outclassed and that he was not beaten by superior skill. One is glad to find that von Richthofen pays a tribute to the bravery and ability of his enemy, and it is perhaps some slight consolation to those of us who knew Lanoe Hawker to think that he fell a victim to the Germans' best man and not to a chance shot from an unworthy foe.

It is rather curious that some time after emphasising the fact that trickery does not pay in air fighting, von

Richthofen should show how trickery does pay by describing his young brother Lothar's trick of pretending to be shot and letting his machine fall apparently out of control, so as to break off a fight with opponents who were above his weight. One is inclined to wonder how many optimistic young air-fighters have reported enemy machines as "driven down out of control," when in reality the wily Hun has only been getting out of the way of harm. The older hands in these days are not easily caught by such a trick, and the High Command refuses to count any victims so claimed unless the performance is verified by independent witnesses either on the ground or aloft.

Another point of interest in von Richthofen's fighting methods is that he states, as a rule, that he opens fire at 50 yards. Distances are hard to judge in the air. The pilot is more likely to under-estimate them than otherwise, just as one does in judging distances at sea. But von Richthofen is probably as good a judge as any, and in this he seems to be stating a plain fact. In these days 50 yards is fairly long range. Some of our own crack fighters prefer 50 feet, if they can get into their favourite positions. Anyhow he shows the unwisdom of opening fire at 1,000 yards, as some inexperienced and excited machine-gunners are rather apt to do.

Von Richthofen is by no means without a sense of humour. His horse-dealing story at the beginning of the book is quite amusing. So is the incident of "surrounding" a perfectly harmless Luxembourg policeman.

Also one likes his appreciation of the rumour of an English rumour – of which one learns for the first time – that his famous red machine was flown by a kind of German Jeanne d'Arc, because "only a girl would sit in so extravagantly painted a machine." One is not quite sure whether he really got hold of a genuine rumour, or whether he invented it as a rather deep piece of sarcasm. 'n either case the Jeanne d'Arc idea is worthy of our half-penny – I beg its pardon, our now a penny – Press at its most brainless.

Singularly English is his jest about his faithful hound "Moritz" – named on account of his ugliness after one of the famous "Max and Moritz" Simian music-hall duo, whose reputation was pan-European. Von Richthofen, in his appreciation of the dog, remarks, "His mother was a beautiful animal, and one of his fathers was pure-bred. I am convinced of that." About as neat a description of what Calverley called "a pure-bred fancy mongrel" as one has met.

Von Richthofen's chaser squadron – or Jägdstaffel, as the Germans call these formations – was the first to be known as a "circus." The famous Bölcke squadron, although a fairly mobile body, the members of which co-operated closely on occasion, never developed formation fighting to the extent that von Richthofen did.

His men, although, as the book shows, they went out periodically on lone-hand ventures, generally flew in a body, numbering anything from half a dozen to fifteen or so. Their leader chose to paint his little Albatros a brilliant pillar-box red. The others painted their machines according to their fancy. Some had yellow noses, blue bodies and green wings. Some were pale blue underneath and black on top. Some were painted in streaks. Some with spots. In fact, they rang the changes on the whole of the paint-box.

They flew wonderfully, being all picked men, and in a fight they performed in a manner which would have seemed impossible to the most expert aerial acrobats of pre-war aerodrome exhibitions.

Also, the squadron was moved from place to place as a self-contained unit, so that it appeared wherever the fighting was thickest, or wherever British or French reconnaissance machines were busiest. It would be operating at Verdun one week. The next week it would be north of Arras. A few days later it would be down on the Somme. But as a rule it specialised on the British front. Wherever it pitched its tents it did its regular squadron performance, and followed it later in the day with lone-hand raids, or "strafing" flight by two or three machines at a time.

When one considers the harlequin colouring of the machines, their acrobatic flying and their "two shows a day" performances from their one-week pitches, it follows logically that the humorists of the R.F.C. simply had to call the squadron "Von Richthofen's Travelling Circus."

Since then the word has acquired a meaning of its own among flying men. It connotes practically any special formation organised for the purpose of hunting enemy aviators, and consisting of picked men under a specially skilful leader. It need not necessarily be more mobile than any other squadron, and it need not indulge in freak colourings, though, in the nature of its work, its flying must be acrobatic. The British "circuses" are in these days superior to the German circuses, because our machines are now at least as good as those of the Germans, and so our men, who have always been of higher average quality than the German aviators, have a fair chance of proving their worth.

Of those of von Richthofen's circus mentioned in the book, Schäfer was the first to be killed. Before the war he lived in London, to learn English, working in an office in the City, when so inclined, but mostly spending his time on the river, or in sport. Those who knew him say that he was a pleasant lad and a good sportsman.

Voss was the next to go, after what has been described by those who were in it as one of the most gallant fights of the war. On a Fokker triplane with a French le Rhône engine – evidently an experimental machine built for quick manœuvring – he fought single-handed a patrol of six of our people, when he could have broken off the fight and have got away by abandoning an inferior companion. He was a brave man and a most brilliant pilot. His flying and shooting in his last fight is said to have been marvellously clever. None admire his bravery more than those who fought him.

Others of the ''circus'' have fallen since then, and the last ''Richthofen Jagdstaffel'' was probably constituted very differently from that band of high-spirited desperadoes which was evolved from the original Bölcke squadron, and helped to build up the fame of von Richthofen.

Manfred von Richthofen himself was killed on April 21, 1918, in a fight over the Valley of the Somme, which he himself described as his happy hunting ground. He was buried with full military honours by his old enemies of the R.F.C., as befitted a gallant gentleman who died for his Fatherland. Let us hope that where he has gone he and his former foes may meet one another as brave men do when peace is declared between them.

There is none of the old R.F.C. who would not cheerfully kill what is left of the ''circus,'' and there is probably none who would not gladly shake hands with the survivors after peace is declared. They are worthy enemies and good fighters.

This little book gives one a useful insight into the enemy's methods, and more than a little respect for at any rate some of those whom we are at present endeavouring to kill.

I

MY FAMILY

THE family of Richthofen has taken no very great part in wars until now. The von Richthofens have always lived in the country. There has scarcely been a von Richthofen without a landed estate. If he did not live in the country he was, as a rule, in the State service. My grandfather and all my ancestors before him had properties about Breslau and Striegau. Only in the generation of my grandfather it happened that the first von Richthofen, his cousin, became a General.

My mother belongs to the family of von Schickfuss und Neudorf. Its character resembles that of the Richthofen people. There were a few soldiers in that family. All the rest were agrarians. The brother of my great-grandfather Schickfuss fell in 1806. During the Revolution of 1848 one of the finest castles of a Schickfuss was burnt down. The Schickfuss have, as a rule, only become Captains of the Reserve.

In the family of Schickfuss and in the family of Falckenhausen – my grandmother's maiden name was Falckenhausen – the two principal hobbies were horse riding and game shooting. My mother's brother, Alexander Schickfuss, has done a great deal of game shooting in Africa, Ceylon, Norway and Hungary.*

My father is practically the first member of our branch of the family who had the idea of becoming a professional soldier. At an early age he entered the Corps of Cadets and joined later the 12th Regiment of Uhlans. He was the most conscientious soldier imaginable. He began to suffer from difficulty of hearing and had to resign. He contracted ear trouble through saving one of his men from drowning, and though he was wet through and through he insisted upon continuing his duties as if nothing had happened, wet as he was, without taking notice of the rigour of the weather. The present generation of the Richthofens contains, of course, many more soldiers. In war every able-bodied Richthofen is, of course, on active service. In the very beginning of "the war of movement" I lost six cousins, and all were in the Cavalry.

I have been named after my uncle Manfred who, in peace time, was Adjutant to His Majesty and Commander of the Corps of the Guards. During the war he has been Commander of a Corps of Cavalry.

My father was in the 1st Regiment of Cuirassiers in Breslau when I was born on the 2nd of May, 1892. We lived then at Kleinburg. I received tuition privately until my ninth year. Then I went for a year to school in Schweidnitz and then I became a Cadet in Wahlstatt. The people of Schweidnitz considered me as one of their own. Having been prepared for a military career as a Cadet, I entered the 1st Regiment of Uhlans.

My own adventures and experiences will be found in this book.

---

*Here we have an example of the force of heredity. The man who is a born horseman is almost always a born aviator. The steadiness of hand and quickness of eye which is necessary to a first-class game shot is equally necessary to the fighting pilot.

My brother Lothar is the other flying-man Richthofen. He wears the Ordre pour le Mérite. My youngest brother is still in the Corps of Cadets and he is waiting anxiously until he is old enough to go on active service. My sister, like all the ladies of our family, is occupied in nursing the wounded.

MY LIFE AS A CADET

(1903-1909 Wahlstatt, 1909-1911 Lichterfelde.)

As a little boy of eleven I entered the Cadet Corps. I was not particularly eager to become a Cadet, but my father wished it. So my wishes were not consulted.

I found it difficult to bear the strict discipline and to keep order. I did not care very much for the instruction I received. I never was good at learning things. I did just enough work to pass. In my opinion it would have been wrong to do more than was just sufficient, so I worked as little as possible. The consequence was that my teachers did not think overmuch of me. On the other hand, I was very fond of sport, particularly I liked my gymnastics, football, etc. I could do all possible tricks on the horizontal bar. So I received soon some prizes from the Commandant.

I had a tremendous liking for all sorts of risky tricks. One fine day I climbed with my friend Frankenberg the well-known steeple of Wahlstatt by means of the lightning conductor and tied my handkerchief to the top. I remember exactly how difficult it was to negotiate the gutters. Ten years later, when I visited my little brother at Wahlstatt, I saw my handkerchief still tied up high in the air.*

*An excellent testimonial to the durability of the fabric or else to his imagination.

41

My friend Frankenberg was the first victim of the war as far as I know.

I liked very much better the Institution of Lichterfelde. I did not feel so isolated from the world, and began to live a little more like a human being.

My happiest reminiscences of Lichterfelde are those of the great sports when my opponent was Prince Friederich Karl.* The Prince gained many first prizes against me in running and so forth, as I had not trained as carefully as he had done.

ENTERING THE ARMY

(Easter, 1911.)

Of course I was very impatient to get into the Army. Immediately after passing my examination I came forward, and was placed in the 1st Regiment of Uhlans ("Emperor Alexander III.") I had selected that regiment. It was garrisoned in my beloved Silesia, and I had there some acquaintances and relations who advised me to join it.

I had a very great liking for the service with my Regiment. It is the finest thing for a young soldier to be a cavalryman.

I can say only little about the time which I passed at the War Academy. My experience there reminds me too much of the Corps of Cadets, and consequently my reminiscences are not over agreeable.

I had a funny experience at the War Academy. One of our instructors bought a very nice fat mare. Her only fault was that she was rather old. She was supposed to be fifteen years old; she had rather stout legs, but she

*Later killed while flying in France.

42

jumped splendidly. I rode her frequently, and her name was Biffy.

About a year later, when I joined the Regiment, my Captain, von Tr—, who was very fond of sport, told me that he had bought a funny little mare, a fat beast, who jumped very nicely. We all were very interested to make the acquaintance of the fat jumping horse who bore the strange name Biffy. I had quite forgotten the old mare of my instructor at the War Academy. One fine morning, the animal arrived and I was astonished to find that the ancient Biffy was now standing as an eight-year-old in the Captain's stable. In the meantime, she had changed her master repeatedly, and had much risen in value. My instructor had bought her for £75 as a fifteen-year old, and von Tr— had bought her a year later as an eight-year-old for £175. She won no more prizes for jumping, but she changed her master once more, and fell in the beginning of the war.

AN OFFICER

(Autumn, 1912.)

At last I was given the epaulettes. It was a glorious feeling, the finest I have ever experienced, when people called me Lieutenant.

My father bought me a beautiful mare called Santuzza. She was a marvellous animal, as hard as nails. She kept her place on parade like a lamb. In course of time, I discovered that she possessed a great talent for jumping, and I made up my mind to train her. She jumped incredible heights. I jumped with her over a metre and a half (nearly 5 feet).

In this enterprise I got much sympathy and co-operation

from my comrade, von Wedel, who won many a prize with his charger Fandango.

We two trained our horses for a jumping competition and a steeplechase at Breslau. Fandango did gloriously. Santuzza also did well by taking a great deal of trouble. I hoped to achieve something with her. On the day before she was to be put on the train I wished once more to jump all the obstacles on our training ground. In doing so we slipped. Santuzza hurt her shoulder and I broke my collar-bone.

I expected that my dear fat mare Santuzza would also be fast on the flat, and was extremely surprised when she was beaten by Wedel's thoroughbred.

Another time I had the good fortune to ride a very fine horse in a Steeplechase at Breslau. My horse did extremely well on a run over about half the course, and I had hopes of succeeding. I approached the last obstacle. At a long distance I saw that the obstacle in front was bound to be something extraordinary, because a great crowd was watching near it. I said to myself: "Keep your courage up. You are sure to get into trouble." I approached the obstacle going full speed. The people about waved to me and shouted that I should not go so fast, but I neither heard nor saw. My horse jumped over, and on the other side there was a steep slope with the river Weistritz in front. Before I could say knife the horse, having jumped, fell with a gigantic leap into the river, and horse and rider disappeared. Of course I was thrown over the head of the horse. Felix got out of the river on the one side and I on the other. When I came back, the weighing people were surprised that I had put on ten pounds instead of losing two pounds as usual. Happily no one noticed that I was wet through and through.

I had also a very good charger. The unfortunate beast had to do everything, racing, steeplechasing, jumping, army service. There was nothing that the poor beast had not learned. His name was Blume, and we had some real successes. The last prize I got riding that horse was when I rode for the Kaiser Prize in 1913.* I was the only one who got over the whole course without a single mistake in direction. In doing so I had an experience which I should not care to repeat. In galloping over a piece of heath land I suddenly stood on my head. The horse had stepped into a rabbit hole, and in my fall I had broken my collar-bone. Notwithstanding the breakage, I rode another forty miles without making a mistake and arrived, keeping good time.**

THE OUTBREAK OF WAR

All the papers contained nothing but fantastic stories about the war. However, for several months all were accustomed to war talk. We had so often packed our service trunk that the whole thing had become tedious. No one believed any longer that there would be war. We who were close to the frontier, who were "the eyes of the Army," to use the words of my Commanding Officer, believed least that there would be war.

On the day before military preparations began we were sitting with the people of the detached squadron at a distance of 10 kilometres from the frontier, in the Officers' Club. We were eating oysters, drinking champagne and gambling a little. We were very merry. No one thought of war.

---

*A long distance ride.
**These horse-coping, horse-racing, and horse-handling reminiscences go far to confirm the belief that a good horseman is almost always a good flier.

True, some days earlier Wedel's mother had startled us a little. She had arrived from Pomerania in order to see her son before the beginning of the war. As she found us in the pleasantest mood, and as she ascertained that we did not think of war, she felt morally compelled to invite us to a very decent lunch.

We were extremely gay and noisy when suddenly the door opened. It disclosed Count Kospoth, the Administrator of Ols. He looked like a ghost.

We greeted our old friend with a loud Hurrah! He explained to us the reason of his arrival. He had come personally to the frontier in order to convince himself whether the rumours of an impending world-war were true. He assumed quite correctly that the best information could be obtained at the frontier. He was not a little surprised when he saw our peaceful assembly. We learned from him that all the bridges in Silesia were being patrolled by the military, and that steps were being taken to fortify various positions.

We convinced him quickly that the possibility of war was absolutely nil, and continued our festivity.

On the next day we were ordered to take the field.

WE CROSS THE FRONTIER

To us cavalrymen on the frontier the word ''war'' had nothing unfamiliar. Everyone of us knew to the smallest detail what to do, and what to leave undone. At the same time, nobody had a very clear idea what the first thing would be. Every soldier was delighted to be able to show his capacity and his personal value.

We young cavalry lieutenants had the most interesting task. We were to study the ground, to work towards the rear of the enemy, and to destroy important objects. All these tasks require real men.

Having in my pocket my directions, and having convinced myself of their importance through hard study during at least a year, I rode at the head of my men for the first time against the enemy at twelve o'clock midnight.

A river marked the frontier, and I expected to be fired upon on reaching it. To my astonishment I passed over the bridge without an incident. On the next morning we reached the church of the village of Kieltze, which was well known to us through our frontier rides, without having had any adventures.

Everything had happened without seeing anything of the enemy, or rather without being seen by him. The question now was, What should I do in order not to be noticed by the villagers? My first idea was to lock up the "pope."* We fetched him from his house, to his great surprise. I locked him up among the bells in the church tower, took away the ladder, and left him sitting up above. I assured him that he would be executed if the population should show any hostile inclinations. A sentinel placed on the tower observed the neighbourhood.

I had to send reports every day by despatch-riders. Very soon my small troop was converted into despatch-riders and dissolved, so that I had at last, as the only one remaining, to bring in my own report.

Up to the fifth night everything had been quiet. During that night the sentinel came suddenly rushing to the church tower near which the horses had been put. He called out:

*Russian priest.

47

"The Cossacks are here!" The night was as dark as pitch. It rained a little. No stars were visible. One could not see a yard ahead.

As a precaution we had previously breached the wall around the churchyard. Through the breach we took the horses into the open. The darkness was so great that we were in perfect security after having advanced fifty yards. I myself went with the sentinel, carbine in hand, to the place where he pretended he had seen Cossacks.

Gliding along the churchyard wall I came to the street. When I got there I experienced a funny feeling, for the street swarmed with Cossacks. I looked over the wall behind which the rascals had put the horses. Most of them had lanterns, and they acted very incautiously and were very noisy. I estimated that they were from twenty to thirty. One had left his horse and gone to the "pope" whom I had let off the day before.

Immediately it flashed through my brain, "Of course we are betrayed!" Therefore, we had to be doubly careful. I could not risk a fight, because I could not dispose of more than two carbines. Therefore, I resolved to play at robber and policeman.

After having rested a few hours, our visitors rode away again.

On the next day I thought it wise to change our quarters. On the seventh day I was again back in my garrison, and everyone stared at me as if I were a ghost. The staring was not due to my unshaved face, but because there had been a rumour that Wedel and I had fallen at Kalisch. The place where it had occurred, the time and all the circumstances of my death had been reported with such a wealth of detail that the report had spread throughout Silesia. My mother had already received visits of condolence. The only thing that had been omitted was an announcement of my death in the newspapers.*

A funny affair happened about the same time. A veterinary surgeon had been ordered to take ten Uhlans and to requisition horses on a farm. The farm was situated about two miles from the road. He came back full of excitement and reported:

"I was riding over a stubble field, the field where the scarecrows are, when I suddenly saw hostile infantry at a distance. Without a moment's hesitation I drew my sword and ordered the Uhlans to attack them with their lances. The men were delighted, and at the fastest gallop they rushed across the field. When we came near the enemy I discovered that the hostile infantry consisted of some deer whom I had mistaken for soldiers owing to my short-sightedness."

For a long time that dear gentleman had to suffer from his attack.**

TO FRANCE

We were ordered to take the train in my garrison town. No one had any idea whether we were to go west, east, south or north.

There were many rumours, but most talk was very wild. However, in this present case we had the right idea: westward.

A second-class compartment had been given to four of us. We had to take in provisions for a long railway journey.

*Which reminds one curiously of the way in which rumours of the wildest yet most circumstantial description flew about in England early in the war.

**This is rather like the experience of a British aviator who flew for miles across Belgium to attack a Zeppelin, only to find that the "airship" was a strip of corn on a hill-top shining in the rays of the setting sun.

Liquid refreshments, of course, were not lacking. However, already on the first day we discovered that a second-class compartment is beastly narrow for four warlike youths. Therefore, we resolved to distribute ourselves. I arranged part of a goods car and converted it into a bed-drawing-room, to my great advantage. I had light, air, etc. I procured straw at one of the stations and put a tent cloth on top of it. In my improvised sleeping car I slept as well as I did in my four-poster in Ostrowo. We travelled night and day, first through Silesia, and then through Saxony, going westward all the time. Apparently we were going in the direction of Metz. Even the train conductor did not know whither he was going.

At every station, even at stations where we did not stop, there were huge crowds of men and women bombarded us with cheers and flowers. The German nation had been seized by a wild war enthusiasm. That was evident. The Uhlans were particularly admired. The men in the train who had passed through the station before us had probably reported that we had met the enemy, and we had been at war only for a week. Besides, my regiment had been mentioned in the first official communiqué. The 1st Regiment of Uhlans and the 155th Regiment of Infantry had taken Kalisch. We were therefore celebrated as heroes, and naturally felt like heroes. Wedel had found a Cossack sword which he showed to admiring girls. He made a great impression with it. Of course we asserted that blood was sticking to it, and we invented hair-raising tales around the peaceful sword of a police officer. We were very wild and merry until we were disembarked from the train at Busendorf, near Diedenhofen.

A short time before the train arrived we were held up in a long tunnel. It is uncomfortable enough to stop in a tunnel in peace time, but to stop suddenly in war is still more uncomfortable. Some excited high-spirited fellow wanted to play a joke and fired a shot. Before long there was general firing in the tunnel. It was surprising that no one was hurt. It has never been found out how the general shooting was brought about.*

At Busendorf we had to get out of the train. The heat was so great that our horses almost collapsed. On the following day we marched unceasingly northward in the direction of Luxemburg. In the meantime I had discovered that my brother had ridden in the same direction with a cavalry division a week before. I discovered his spoor once more, but I did not see him until a year later.

Arrived in Luxemberg no one knew what were our relations with the people of that little State. When I saw a Luxemburg policeman from a long distance I surrounded him with a file of men and meant to make him a prisoner. He told me that he would complain about me to the German Emperor if I did not set him free immediately. I thought there was reason in what he said. So I let him go. We passed through the City of Luxemburg and through Esch, and we approached the first fortified towns of Belgium.

While advancing, our Infantry, and indeed our whole Division, manœuvred exactly as in peace time. All were extremely excited. It was a good thing that we had to act exactly as we had done at manœuvres, otherwise, we should certainly have done some wild things. To the right and to the left of us, before and behind us, on every road, marched troops belonging to different Army Corps. One had the feeling that everything was in a great disorder. Suddenly, this unspeakable huddle-muddle was dissolved and became a most wonderfully arranged evolution.

I had no idea about the activity of our flying men. At any

*Which is quite unlike the alleged stolid German.

rate, I got tremendously excited whenever I saw an aviator. Of course I had not the slightest idea whether it was a German airman or an enemy. I had at that time not even the knowledge that the German machines were marked with crosses and the enemy machines with circles. The consequence was that every aeroplane we saw was fired upon. Our old pilots are still telling all and sundry of their painful feelings while being shot at by friend and enemy with perfect impartiality.*

We marched and marched, sending patrols far ahead, until we arrived at Arlon. I had a funny feeling when crossing for a second time an enemy frontier. Obscure reports of *franc tireurs*, etc., had already come to my ears.

I had been ordered to work in connection with my cavalry division, acting as a connecting link. On that day I had ridden no less than 66 miles** with my men. Not a horse cracked up. That was a splendid achievement. At Arlon I climbed the steeple in accordance with the tactical principles which we had been taught in peace time. Of course I saw nothing, for the wicked enemy was still far away.

At that time we were very harmless. For instance, I had left my men outside the town, and had ridden along on a bicycle right through the town to the church tower, and ascended it. When I came down again I was surrounded by a crowd of angry young men who made hostile eyes, and who talked threateningly in undertones. My bicycle had, of course, been punctured, and I had to go on foot for half an hour. This incident amused me. I should have been delighted had it come to a fight. I felt absolutely sure of myself with a pistol in my hand.

*This was exactly the experience of British aviators in the early days of war.
**This seems almost unbelievable. At any rate the horses can have been of little use for some days afterwards.

Later on I heard that the inhabitants had behaved very treacherously several days previously towards our cavalry, and later on towards our ambulances. It had therefore been found necessary to place quite a number of these gentlemen against the wall.

In the afternoon I reached the station where I had to go, and learned that close to Arlon my only Richthofen cousin had been killed three days before. During the rest of the day I stayed with the Cavalry Division. During the night a causeless alarm took place, and late at night I reached my own regiment.

Having already been in touch with the enemy and having seen something of war we cavalrymen were envied by the men of the other arms. That was a beautiful time. For me it was the most beautiful time during the whole of the war. I would much like to pass again through the beginning of the war.

THE WHISTLING OF THE FIRST BULLETS

(21-22nd August, 1914.)

I had been ordered to find out the strength of the enemy occupying the large forest near Virton. I started with fifteen Uhlans, and said to myself: "To-day I shall have the first fight with the enemy." But my task was not easy. In so big a forest there may be lots of things hidden which one cannot see.

I went to the top of a little hill. A few hundred paces in front of me was a huge forest extending over many thousands of acres. It was a beautiful August morning. The forest seemed so peaceful and still that I almost forgot all my warlike ideas.

53

We approached the margin of the forest. As we could not discover anything suspicious with our field-glasses we had to go near and find out whether we should be fired upon. The men in front were swallowed up by a forest lane. I followed, and at my side was one of my best Uhlans. At the entrance to the forest was a lonely forester's cottage. We rode past it.

The soil indicated that a short time previously considerable numbers of hostile cavalry must have passed. I stopped my men, encouraged them by addressing a few words to them, and felt sure that I could absolutely rely upon everyone of my soldiers. Of course no one thought of anything except of attacking the enemy. It lies in the instinct of every German to rush at the enemy wherever he meets him, particularly if he meets hostile cavalry. In my mind's eye I saw myself at the head of my little troop sabring a hostile squadron, and was quite intoxicated with joyful expectation. The eyes of my Uhlans sparkled. Thus we followed the spoor at a rapid trot. After a sharp ride of an hour through the most beautiful mountain dale the wood became thinner. We approached the exit. I felt convinced that there we should meet the enemy. Therefore, caution! To the right of our narrow path was a steep rocky wall many yards high. To the left, a narrow rivulet, and at the further side a meadow, 50 yards wide, surrounded by barbed wire. Suddenly the trace horses' hoofs disappeared over a bridge into the bushes. My leading men stopped because the exit from the forest was blocked by a barricade.

Immediately I recognised that I had fallen into a trap. I saw a movement among the bushes behind the meadow at my left, and noticed dismounted hostile cavalry. I estimated that they were 100 rifles. In that direction nothing could be done. My path right ahead was cut by the barricade. To the right were steep rocks. To the left the barbed wire surrounded the meadow, and prevented me attacking as I had intended. Nothing was to be done except to go back. I knew that my dear Uhlans would be willing to do everything except to run away from the enemy. That spoilt our fun, for a second later we heard the first shot, which was followed by very intensive rifle fire from the wood. The distance was from 50 to 100 yards.

I had told my men to join me immediately when they saw me lifting up my hand. I felt sure we had to go back. So I lifted my arm and beckoned my men to follow. Possibly they misunderstood my gesture. The horsemen who were following me believed me in danger, and they came rushing along at a great speed to help me to get away. As we were on a narrow forest path one can imagine the muddle which followed. The horses of the two men ahead rushed away in a panic because the noise of every shot was increased ten-fold by the narrowness of the hollow way. The last I saw of them was that they were leaping the barricade. I never heard anything of them again. They were no doubt made prisoners. I myself turned my horse and gave him the spurs, probably for the first time during his life. I had the greatest difficulty to make the Uhlans who rushed towards me understand that they should not advance any further, that we were to turn round and get away. My orderly rode at my side. Suddenly his horse was hit and fell. I jumped over them, and horses were rolling all around me. In short, it was a wild disorder.

The last I saw of my orderly was that he was lying under his horse, apparently not wounded, but pinned down by the weight of the animal. The enemy had beautifully surprised us. He had probably observed us from the very beginning, and had intended to trap us and to catch us unawares as is the character of the French.

I was delighted when, two days later, I saw my orderly standing before me. He wore only one boot, for he had left the other one under the body of his horse. He told me how he had escaped. At least two squadrons of French cuirassiers had issued from the forest in order to plunder the fallen horses and the brave Uhlans. Not being wounded, he had jumped up, climbed the rocks, and had fallen down exhausted among the bushes. About two hours later, when the enemy had again hidden himself, he had continued his flight. So he had joined me after some days, but he could tell me little about the fate of his comrades who had been left behind.*

A RIDE WITH LOEN

The battle of Virton was proceeding. My comrade Loen and I had once more to ascertain what had become of the enemy. We rode after the enemy during the whole of the day, reached him at last, and were able to write a very decent report. In the evening the great question was: Shall we go riding throughout the night in order to join our troops, or shall we economise our strength and take a rest so that we shall be fresh the next day? The splendid thing about cavalrymen on patrol is that they are given complete liberty of action.

We resolved to pass the night near the enemy, and to ride on the next morning. According to our strategical notions, the enemy was retiring and we were following him. Consequently we could pass the night with fair security.

Not far from the enemy there was a wonderful monastery with large stables. So both Loen and I had quarters for

*This strikes one as a very honest description by the victim of a very complete ambush. It shows the carelessness with which the Germans conducted the war in its earlier stages.

ourselves and our men. Of course, in the evening, when we entered our new domicile, the enemy was so near that he could have shot us through the windows.

The monks were extremely amiable. They gave us as much to eat and to drink as we cared to have, and we had a very good time. The saddles were taken off the horses, and they were very happy when, for the first time for three days and three nights, a dead weight of 20 stone was taken from their backs. We settled down as if we were on manœuvres, and as if we were in the house of a delightful host and friend. At the same time it should be observed that three days later we hanged several of our hosts to the lanterns because they could not overcome their desire to take a hand in the war. But that evening they were really extremely amiable. We got into our nightshirts, jumped into bed, posted a sentinel, and let the Lord look after us.

In the middle of the night somebody suddenly flung open the door and shouted: "Sir, the French are here!" I was too sleepy and too heavy to be able to reply. Loen, who was similarly incapacitated, gave the most intelligent answer: "How many are they?" The soldier stammered, full of excitement, "We have shot dead two, but we cannot say how many they are, for it is pitch dark." I heard Loen reply, in a sleepy tone: "All right. When more are arriving call me again." Half a minute later both of us continued snoring.

The next morning the sun was already high in the horizon when we woke up from a refreshing sleep. We took an ample breakfast, and then continued our journey.

As a matter of fact, the French had passed by our castle during the night and our sentinels had fired on them. As it was a very dark night nothing further followed.

Soon we passed through a pretty valley. We rode over the battlefield of our Division and discovered, to our surprise, that it was peopled not with German soldiers, but with

French Red Cross men. Here and there were French soldiers. They looked as surprised at seeing us as we did at seeing them. Nobody thought of shooting. We cleared out as rapidly as possible, and gradually it dawned upon us that our troops, instead of advancing, had retired. Fortunately, the enemy had retired at the same time in the opposite direction. Otherwise I should now be somewhere in captivity.

We passed through the village of Robelmont, where we had seen our Infantry on the previous day in occupation. We encountered one of the inhabitants and asked him what had become of our soldiers. He looked very happy, and assured me that the Germans had departed.

Late in the afternoon I reached my regiment, and was quite satisfied with the course of events during the last twenty-four hours.

BOREDOM BEFORE VERDUN

I am a restless spirit. Consequently my inactivity in front of Verdun can only be described as boresome. At the beginning I was in the trenches at a spot where nothing happened. Then I became a despatch-bearer and hoped to have some adventures. But there I was mistaken. The fighting men immediately despised me and considered me a "Basehog." I was not really at the Base, but I was not allowed to advance further than within 1,500 yards behind the front trenches. There, below the ground, I had a bomb-proof, heated habitation. Now and then I had to go to the front trenches. That was a great physical exertion, for one had to trudge uphill and downhill, criss-cross, through an unending number of trenches and mire-holes until at last one arrived at a place where men were firing. After having paid a short visit to the fighting men, my position seemed to me a very stupid one.

At that time the digging business was beginning. It had not yet become clear to us what it means to dig approaches, etc. Of course we knew the names of various ditches and holes through the lessons which we had received at the War Academy. However, the digging was considered to be the business of the military engineers. Other troops were supposed not to take a hand in it.* However, here near Combres, everyone was digging industriously. Every soldier had a spade and a pick, and took all imaginable trouble in order to get as deeply into the ground as possible. It was very funny that in many places the French were only five yards ahead of us. One could hear them speak and see them smoke cigarettes, and now and then they threw us a piece of paper. We conversed with them, but nevertheless we tried to annoy them in every possible way, especially with hand grenades.

Five hundred yards in front of us and five hundred yards behind the trenches the dense forest of the Côte Lorraine had been cut down by the vast number of shells and bullets which unceasingly were being fired. It seemed unbelievable that in front men could live. Nevertheless, the men in the front trenches were not in as bad a position as the men at the Base.

After a morning visit to the front trenches, which usually took place at the earliest hours of the day, the more tedious business began. I had to attend to the telephone.

On days when I was off duty I indulged in my favourite pastime, game shooting. The forest of La Chaussée gave me ample opportunities. When going for a ride I had noticed that there were wild pigs about, and I tried to find out where I could shoot them at night. Beautiful nights,

*This hardly coincides with the popular idea of the high development of German military science and of German preparedness before the war.

with a full moon and snow, came to my aid. With the assistance of my servants I built a shelter seat in a tree at a spot where the pigs passed, and waited there at night. Thus I passed many a night sitting on the branch of a tree, and on the next morning found that I had become an icicle. However, I got my reward. There was a sow which was particularly interesting. Every night she swam across the lake, broke into a potato field, always at the same spot, and then she swam back again. Of course I very much wished to improve my acquaintance with the animal. So I took a seat on the other shore of the lake. In accordance with our previous arrangement, Auntie Pig appeared at midnight for her supper. I shot her while she was still swimming, and she would have been drowned had I not succeeded at the last moment in seizing her by the leg.

At another time I was riding with my servant along a narrow path. Suddenly I saw several wild pigs crossing it. Immediately I jumped from the horse, grasped my servant's carbine and rushed several hundred yards ahead. At the end of the procession, came a mighty boar. I had never yet seen such a beast, and was surprised at its gigantic size. Now it ornaments my room and reminds me of my encounter.

In this manner I had passed several months when, one fine day, our shop became busy. We intended a small attack. I was delighted, for now at last I should be able to do something as a connecting link. But there came another disappointment! I was given quite a different job, and now I had enough of it. I sent a letter to my Commanding General, and evil tongues reported that I said to him: "My dear Excellency! I have not gone to war in order to collect cheese and eggs, but for another purpose." At first, the people above wanted to snarl at me. But then they fulfilled my wish. Thus I joined the Flying Service at the end of May, 1915. My greatest wish was fulfilled.

II

FOR THE FIRST TIME IN THE AIR

THE next morning at seven o'clock I was to fly for the first time as an observer! I was naturally very excited, for I had no idea what it would be like. Everyone whom I had asked about his feelings told me a different tale. The night before I went earlier to bed than usual in order to be thoroughly refreshed the next morning. We drove over to the flying ground, and I got for the first time into a flying machine. The draught from the propeller was a beastly nuisance. I found it quite impossible to make myself understood by the pilot. Everything was carried away by the wind. If I took up a piece of paper it disappeared. My safety helmet slid off. My muffler dropped off. My jacket was not sufficiently buttoned. In short, I felt very uncomfortable. Before I knew what was happening, the pilot went ahead at full speed, and the machine started rolling. We went faster and faster. I clutched the sides of the car. Suddenly, the shaking was over, the machine was in the air and the earth dropped away from under me.

I had been told where we were to fly to. I was to direct my pilot. At first we flew right ahead, then my pilot turned to the right, then to the left, but I had lost all sense of direction above our own aerodrome. I had not the slightest notion where I was. I began very cautiously to look over the side at the country. The men looked ridiculously small. The houses seemed to come out of a child's toy box. Everything seemed pretty. Cologne was in the background. The cathedral looked like a little toy. It was a glorious feeling to be so high above the earth, to be master of the air. I didn't care a bit where I was, and I felt extremely sorry when my pilot thought it was time to go down again.

I should have liked best to start immediately on another flight. I have never had any trouble in the air, such as vertigo. The popular "American swings" are to me disgusting. One does not feel secure in them. But in a flying machine one possesses a feeling of complete security. One sits in an aeroplane as in an easy chair. Vertigo is impossible. No man exists who has been turned giddy by flying. At the same time, flying affects one's nerves when one races full speed through the air, and particularly when one goes down again, when the aeroplane suddenly dips, when the engine stops running, and when the tremendous noise is followed by an equally tremendous silence. Again, one frantically clutches the sides and thinks "Of course, now you fall to the ground!" However, everything happens in such a matter of fact and natural way, and the landing, when one again touches *terra firma*, is so simple, that one could not have such a feeling as fear. I was full of enthusiasm, and would have liked to be sitting in an aeroplane all day long. I counted the hours to the next start.

AS AN OBSERVER WITH MACKENSEN

On the 10th of June, 1915, I came to Grossenhain. Thence I was to be sent to the front. Of course I was anxious to go forward as quickly as possible. I feared that I might come too late, that the world-war might be over. I should have had to spend three months to become a pilot. By the time the three months had gone by, peace might have been concluded. Therefore, it never occurred to me to become a pilot. I imagined that, owing to my training as a cavalryman, I might do well as an observer. I was very happy when, after a fortnight's flying experience, I was sent out,* and that I was sent to the only spot where there was still a chance of a war of movement. I was sent to Russia.

Mackensen was advancing gloriously. He had broken through the Russian position at Gorlice, and I joined his Army when we were taking Rawa Ruska. I spent a day at the aviation base, and then I was sent to the celebrated 69th Squadron. Being quite a beginner I felt very foolish. My pilot was a big gun, Ober-Lieutenant Zeumer. He is now a cripple. Of the other men of the section I am the only survivor.

Now came my most beautiful time. Life in the Flying Corps is very much like life in the Cavalry. Every day, morning and afternoon, I had to fly and to reconnoitre, and I have brought back many a time valuable information.

WITH HOLCK IN RUSSIA

(Summer, 1915.)

During June, July and August, 1915, I remained with the Flying Service which participated in Mackensen's advance from Gorlice to Brest-Litovsk. I had joined it as quite a juvenile observer and had not the slightest idea of anything.

---

*At a fair estimate this would mean between 12 and 15 hours in the air, so that evidently the highly organised, methodical Germans rushed their air training in the same haphazard way as did the British R.F.C. in those early days.

As a cavalryman my business had consisted in reconnoitring. So the Flying Service as an observer was in my line, and it amused me vastly to take part in the gigantic reconnoitring flights which we undertook nearly every day.

For an observer it is important to find a pilot with a strong character.* One fine day we were told "Count Holck will join us." Immediately I had the idea, "That is the man I want."

Holck made his appearance not, as one would imagine, in a 60 h.p. Mercedes or in a first-class sleeping car. He came on foot. After travelling by railway for days and days he had arrived in the vicinity of Jaroslav. Here he got out of the train, for there was once more an unending stoppage. He told his servant to travel on with the luggage while he would go on on foot. He marched along and after an hour's walking looked back, but the train did not follow him. So he walked and walked and walked without being overtaken by the train, until, after a thirty-mile walk, he arrived in Rawa Ruska, his object. Twenty-four hours later his orderly appeared with the luggage. His thirty-mile walk proved no difficulty to that sportsman. His body was so well trained that he did not feel the tramp he had undertaken.

Count Holck was not only a sportsman on land. Flying also was to him a sport which gave him the greatest pleasure. He was a pilot of rare talent, and particularly, and that is after all the principal thing, he towered head and shoulders above the enemy.

We went on many a beautiful reconnoitring flight, I do not know how far, into Russia. Although Holck was so young I had never a feeling of insecurity with him. On the

*It would be interesting to know whether von Richthofen had already discovered this important fact, or whether this is the result of his later experience. In all the war there were none to be more pitied than a good observer who is allocated to a pilot of weak character.

contrary, he was always a support to me in critical moments. When I looked around and saw his determined face I had always twice as much courage as I had had before.

My last flight with him nearly led to trouble. We had not had definite orders to fly. The glorious thing in the flying service is that one feels that one is a perfectly free man and one's own master as soon as one is up in the air.

We had to change our aerodrome and we were not quite certain in which meadow we were to land. In order not to expose our old box* to too much risk in landing we flew in the direction of Brest-Litovsk. The Russians were retiring everywhere. The whole countryside was burning. A terribly beautiful picture. We intended to ascertain the direction of the enemy columns, and in doing so flew over the burning town of Wicznice. A gigantic smoke cloud, which went up to about 6,000 ft., prevented us from continuing our flight because we flew at an altitude of only 4,500 feet in order to see better. For a moment Holck reflected. I asked him what he intended to do and advised him to fly around the smoke cloud, which would have involved a roundabout way of five minutes. Holck did not intend to do this. On the contrary. The greater the danger, the more the thing attracted him. Therefore straight through! I enjoyed it too to be together with such a daring fellow. Our venturesomeness nearly cost us dear. As soon as the tail-end of the machine had disappeared in the smoke the aeroplane began to reel. I could not see a thing, for the smoke made my eyes water. The air was much warmer, and beneath me I saw nothing but a huge sea of fire. Suddenly the machine lost its balance and fell, turning round and round. I managed to grasp a stay and

---

*A literal translation of German aviator's slang corresponding to the bad British habit of calling an aeroplane a "bus."

hung on to it. Otherwise I would have been thrown out of the machine. The first thing I did was to look at Holck, and immediately I regained my courage, for his face showed an iron confidence. The only thought which I had was: "It is stupid after all to die so unnecessarily a hero's death."*

Later on I asked Holck what had been his thoughts at the moment. He told me he had never experienced so unpleasant a feeling.

We fell down to an altitude of 1,500 feet above the burning town. Either through the skill of my pilot or by a Higher Will, perhaps by both, we suddenly dropped out of the smoke cloud. Our good Albatros found itself again and once more flew straight ahead as if nothing had happened.

We had now had enough of it, and instead of going to a new base intended to return to our old quarter as quickly as possible. After all we were still above the Russians and only at an altitude of 1,500 feet. Five minutes later I heard behind me Holck exclaiming: "The motor is giving out."

I must add that Holck had not as much knowledge of motors as he had of horseflesh, and I had not the slightest idea of mechanics. The only thing which I knew was that we should have to land among the Russians if the motor went on strike. So one peril had followed the other.

I convinced myself that the Russians beneath us were still marching with energy. I could see that quite clearly from our low altitude. Besides it was not necessary to look, for the Russians shot at us with machine-guns with the utmost diligence. It sounded like chestnuts frying near a fire.

Presently the motor stopped running altogether, for it had been hit. So we went lower and lower. We just managed to glide over a forest and landed at last in an

*The objection to being a hero unnecessarily is very sound. Many a good man would be alive and useful to-day if this principle had been inculcated into our young aviators.

abandoned artillery position which the evening before had still been occupied by Russians, as I had reported.

I told Holck my impressions. We jumped out of our box and tried to rush into the forest near by, where we might have defended ourselves. I had with me a pistol and six cartridges. Holck had nothing.

When we had reached the wood we stopped and I saw with my glasses that a soldier was running towards our aeroplane. I was horrified to see that he wore not a spiked helmet but a cap. So I felt sure that he was a Russian. When the man came nearer Holck shouted with joy, for he was a Grenadier of the Prussian Guard.

Our élite troops had once more stormed the position at the break of day and had broken through into the enemy batteries.

On that occasion Holck lost his particular pet dog. He took the little animal with him in every night. The dog would lie always quietly on Holck's fur in the fuselage. He was still with us when we were in the forest. Soon after, when we had talked with the Guardsman, German troops passed us. They were the Staffs of the Guard and of Prince Eitel Friedrich with his A.D.C.'s and his Orderly-Officers. The Prince supplied us with horses so that we two cavalry-men were sitting once more on oat-driven motors. Unfortunately, the dog was lost while we were riding. Probably he followed other troops by mistake.

Later in the evening we arrived in our old aerodrome on a cart. The machine was smashed.

RUSSIA–OSTEND

(From the Two-Seater to the Twin-Engined
Fighter)

The German enterprise in Russia came gradually to a stop and suddenly I was transferred to a Big Fighting Machine at Ostend on the 21st August, 1915. There I met an old acquaintance, friend Zeumer. Besides I was attracted by the tempting name "Big Fighting Machine."*

In August, 1915, I arrived in Ostend. Friend Zeumer met me at Brussels station. I had a very nice time. I saw little of the War, but my experiences were invaluable to me, for I passed my apprenticeship as an air fighter. We flew a great deal, we had rarely a fight in the air and we had no successes. We had seized an hotel on the Ostend shore. We bathed every afternoon. Unfortunately the only frequenters of the watering-place were soldiers. Wrapped up in our many-coloured bathing gowns we sat on the terraces of Ostend and drank our coffee in the afternoon.†

One fine day we were sitting as usual on the shore drinking coffee. Suddenly we heard bugles. We were told that an English Naval Squadron was approaching. Of course we did not allow ourselves to be alarmed or disturbed and continued drinking our coffee. Suddenly somebody called out: "There they are!" Indeed we could see on the horizon, though not very distinctly, some smoking funnels and later on could make out ships. Immediately we fetched our telescopes and observed them. There was indeed quite an imposing number of vessels. It was not quite clear to us

---

*The Grossfleugzeug, or "G" class of German aeroplane, later given up as a fighting machine owing to its slow speed and clumsiness in manœuvre and used in its later developments for night-bombing only.

†Another disillusionment concerning the machine-made, strictly disciplined German.

what they intended to do, but soon we were to know better. We went up to the roof whence we could see more.

Suddenly we heard a whistling in the air, then a big bang and a shell hit that part of the beach where a little before we had been bathing. I have never rushed as rapidly into the "heroes' cellar" as I did at that moment. The English Squadron shot perhaps three or four times at us, and then it began bombarding the harbour and railway station. Of course they hit nothing, but they gave a terrible fright to the brave Belgians. One shell fell right in the beautiful Palace Hotel on the shore. That was the only damage that was done. Happily, they destroyed only English capital, for it belonged to Englishmen.

In the evening we flew again with energy. On one of our flights we had gone very far across the sea with our fighting machine. It had two motors and we were experimenting with a new steering gear which, we were told, would enable us to fly in a straight line with only a single motor working.* When we were fairly far out I saw beneath us, not on the water but below the surface, a ship. It is a funny thing. If the sea is calm one can from above look down to the bottom of the water. Of course it is not possible where the sea is twenty-five miles deep, but one can see clearly through several hundred yards of water. I had not made a mistake in believing that the ship was travelling not on the surface but below the surface. Yet it seemed at first that it was travelling above water. I drew Zeumer's attention to my discovery and we went lower in order to see more clearly. I am too little of a naval expert to say what it was, but it was clear to me that it was bound to be a submarine. But of what nationality? That is a difficult question, which in my opinion can be solved

---

*This apparently refers to an auto-lock arrangement on the rudder-bar to save the pilot from having to push the rudder over against the engine all the time.

only by a naval expert, and not always by him. One can scarcely distinguish colours and there is no flag. Besides a submarine does not carry such things. We had with us a couple of bombs and I debated with myself whether I should throw them or not. The submarine had not seen us, for it was partly submerged. We might have flown above it without danger and we might have waited until it found it necessary to come to the surface for air. Then we might have dropped our eggs. Herein lies, no doubt, a very critical point for our sister arm.

When we had fooled around the apparition beneath us for quite a while I suddenly noticed that the water was gradually disappearing from our cooling apparatus. I did not like that, and I drew my colleague's attention to the fact. He pulled a long face and hastened to get home. However, we were approximately twelve miles from the shore and that distance had to be flown. The motor began running more slowly and I was quietly preparing myself for a sudden cold immersion. But lo and behold, we got through! Our giant apple-barge* lumbered along with a single motor and the new steering apparatus, and we reached the shore and managed to land at home.

It is a good thing to be lucky. Had we not tried on that day the new steering apparatus there would not have been any hope for us. We should certainly have been drowned.

---

*Another example of picturesque German slang, analogous more or less to the British term box-kite.

A DROP OF BLOOD FOR THE FATHERLAND

(Ostend.)

I have never been really wounded. At the critical moment I have probably bent my head or pulled in my chest. Often I have been surprised that someone did not hit me. Once a bullet went through both my fur-lined boots. Another time a bullet went through my muffler. Another time one went along my arm through the fur and the leather jacket, but I have never been touched.

One fine day we started with our Big Fighting Machine in order to delight the English with our bombs. We reached our object. The first bomb fell. It is of course very interesting to ascertain the effect of a bomb. At least one always likes to see it explode.

Unfortunately my large machine, which was very well qualified for carrying bombs, had the stupid peculiarity that one could scarcely see the effect of a bomb-throw for the machine came after the throw between one's eye and the object, and covered it completely with its planes. This always made me wild, because one does not like to be deprived of one's amusement. If one hears a bang down below and one sees the delightful greyish-whitish cloud of the explosion in the neighbourhood of the object aimed at one is always very pleased. Therefore I waved to friend Zeumer that he should turn a little to one side. While waving to him I forgot that the infamous object on which I was travelling, my apple-barge, had two air-screws which turned to the right and left of my observer-seat.* I meant to

*From this disposition of the air-screws, and from the date of the occurrence, one assumes that this was one of the very earliest twin-engined Gothas, or A.E.G.'s, of the tractor type which the R.F.C. nicknamed "Wong-wong," because of the curious noise made by the engines or air-screws when they ran out of step.

WEST BRIDGEWATER PUBLIC LIBRARY
80 HOWARD ST.
WEST BRIDGEWATER, MA 02379

show him where approximately the bomb had hit, and, bang! my finger was caught! I was a little surprised when I discovered that my little finger had been damaged. Zeumer did not notice anything.

Having been hit on the hand I did not care for throwing further bombs. I quickly got rid of the lot and we hurried home. My love for the big machine, which after all had not been very great, suffered seriously in consequence of my experience. I had to sit quiet for seven days and was debarred from flying. Only my beauty was slightly damaged, but after all I can say with pride that I also have been wounded in the War.

MY FIRST FIGHT IN THE AIR

(1st Sept., 1915.)

Zeumer and I would have liked very much to have a fight in the air. Of course we flew our Big Fighting Machine. The title of our barge alone gave us so much courage that we thought it impossible for any opponent to escape us.

We flew every day from five to six hours without ever having seen an Englishman. I became quite discouraged, but one fine morning we again went out to hunt. Suddenly I discovered a Farman aeroplane which was reconnoitring without taking notice of us. My heart was beating when Zeumer flew towards it. I was curious to see what was going to happen. I had never witnessed a fight in the air and had about as vague an idea of it as have you, my dear reader.

Before I knew what was happening both the Englishman and I had rushed by one another. I had at most fired four shots while the Englishman was suddenly in our rear firing into our shop window* like anything. I must say I had never the sense of danger because I had no idea how the final result of such a fight would come about. We turned and turned around one another until at last the Englishman, to our great surprise, turned away from us and flew off. I was greatly disappointed, and so was my pilot.

Both of us were in very bad spirits when we reached home. He reproached me for having shot badly, and I reproached him for not having enabled me to shoot well. In short, our aeroplanic relations, which previously had been faultless, had suffered severely.†

We looked at our old box and discovered that it had received quite a respectable number of hits.

On the same day we went on the chase for a second time but again we had no success. I felt very sad. I had imagined that things would be very different in a Battle Squadron. I had always believed that a shot would cause the enemy to fall, but soon I became convinced that a flying machine can stand a great deal of punishment. Finally I felt assured that I should never bring down a hostile aeroplane however much shooting I did.

We did not lack courage. Zeumer was a wonderful flier and I was quite a good shot. We stood before a riddle. We were not the only ones to be puzzled. Many are nowadays in the same position in which we were then. After all, the flying business must really be thoroughly understood.**

---

*Yet another slang term, apparently indicating the body, or fuselage.

†"One touch of nature," etc. How many British pilots and observers have almost come to blows in the air over precisely the same argument?

**Hence the institution of gunnery schools, fighting schools, and so forth. Once more it becomes evident that the Germans were in no way before us in knowledge at this or any other period. Only in the prompt introduction of new types of machines on active service have they ever had any real advantage.

73

IN THE CHAMPAGNE BATTLE

The beautiful time at Ostend was only very short, for soon the Champagne battle began and we flew to the front in order to take part in it in our Big Fighting Machine. Soon we discovered that our packing-case* was no doubt a capacious aeroplane, but that it could never be turned into a good fighting apparatus.

I flew once with Osteroth, who had a smaller flier than the apple-barge. About three miles behind the front we encountered a Farman two-seater. He allowed us to approach him, and for the first time in my life I saw an aerial opponent at close quarters. Osteroth flew with great skill side by side with him so that I could easily fire at him. Our opponent probably did not notice us, for only when I had trouble with my gun did he begin to shoot at us.

When I had exhausted my supply of 100 cartridges I thought I could not trust my eyes when I suddenly noticed that my opponent was going down in curious spirals. I followed him with my eyes and tapped Osteroth's head to draw his attention. Our opponent fell and fell and dropped at last into a large crater. There he was standing on his head, the tail pointing towards the sky. According to the map he had fallen three miles behind the front. We had therefore brought him down on enemy ground. At that time no notice was taken of aeroplanes brought down on enemy ground. †Otherwise I should have one more aeroplane to my credit. I was very proud of my success. After all, the chief thing is to bring a fellow down. It does not matter at all whether one is credited with it or not.

*Still another example of slang, indicative of the clumsiness of the Grossflugzeug in the air.

†It was also the British custom to ignore – as part of the score – all machines brought down in enemy territory. Later it became permissible to count such victims if their destruction was verified by independent witnesses.

III

HOW I MET BOELCKE

FRIEND Zeumer got a Fokker monoplane. Therefore I had to sail through the world alone. The Champagne battle was raging. The French flying men were coming to the fore. We were to be combined in a Fighting Squadron and took train on the 1st October, 1915.

In the dining car, at the table next to me, was sitting a young and insignificant-looking lieutenant. There was no reason to take any note of him except for the fact that he was the only man who had succeeded in shooting down a hostile flying-man, not once but four times. His name had been mentioned in the despatches. I thought a great deal of him because of his experience. Although I had taken the greatest trouble I had not brought an enemy down up to that time. At least I had not been credited with a success.

I would have liked so much to find out how Lieutenant Boelcke managed his business. So I asked him: "Tell me, how do you manage it?" He seemed very amused and laughed, although I had asked him quite seriously. Then he replied: "Well it is quite simple. I fly close to my man, aim well and then of course he falls down."* I shook my head

*This is still the best advice to all who have fancy notions on air fighting.

75

and told him that I did the same thing, but my opponents unfortunately did not come down. The difference between him and me was that he flew a Fokker and I my big fighting machine.

I took great trouble to get more closely acquainted with that nice modest fellow whom I badly wanted to teach me his business. We often played cards together, went for walks, and I asked him questions. At last I formed the resolution that I also would learn to fly a Fokker. Perhaps then my chances would improve.

My whole aim and ambition became now concentrated upon learning how to manipulate the stick myself. Hitherto I had been nothing but an observer. Happily I soon found an opportunity to learn piloting on an old box in the Champagne. I threw myself into the work with body and soul, and after twenty-five training flights I stood before the examination in flying alone.

MY FIRST SOLO-FLIGHT

(10th Oct., 1915.)

There are some moments in one's life which tickle one's nerves particularly, and the first solo-flight is among them.

One fine evening my teacher Zeumer told me: "Now go and fly by yourself." I must say I felt like replying, "I am afraid." But this is a word which should never be used by a man who defends his country. Therefore, whether I liked it or not, I had to swallow it and get into the machine.

Zeumer explained to me once more every movement in theory. I scarcely listened to his explanations, for I was firmly convinced that I should forget half he was telling me.

I started the machine. The aeroplane went at the prescribed speed and I could not help noticing that I was actually flying. After all I did not feel timorous, but rather elated. Now I did not care for anything. I would not have been frightened whatever had happened. With contempt of death I made a large curve to the left, stopped the engine near a tree, exactly where I had been ordered to do so, and looked forward to what would happen. Now came the most difficult thing, the landing. I remembered exactly what movements I had to make. I acted mechanically and the machine moved quite differently from what I had expected. I lost my balance, made some wrong movements, stood on my head and I succeeded in converting my aeroplane into a battered school 'bus.*

I was very sad, looked at the damage which I had done to the machine, which after all was not very great, and had to suffer from other people's jokes.

Two days later I went with passion at the flying and suddenly I could handle the apparatus.

A fortnight later I had to pass my first examination. Herr von T. was my examiner. I described several times the figure eight, exactly as I had been told to do, landed several times with success in accordance with orders received, and felt very proud about my achievements. However, to my great surprise I was told that I had not passed. There was nothing to be done but to try once more to pass the initial examination.

*One likes the neatly humorous description of this first flight solus. Many readers will remember that horrible moment when they have essayed their first turn alone.

MY TRAINING TIME AT DÖBERITZ

In order to pass my examinations I had to go to Berlin. I made use of the opportunity to go to Berlin as observer in a Giant Aeroplane.* I was ordered to go by aeroplane to Döberitz, near Berlin, on the 15th November 1915. In the beginning I took a great interest in the giant aeroplane. But funnily enough, the gigantic machine made it clear to me that only the smallest aeroplane would be of any use for me in battle. A big aerial barge is too clumsy for fighting. Agility is needed, and after all fighting is my business.

The difference between a Big Fighting Machine and a Giant Aeroplane is that a giant aeroplane is considerably larger than a big fighting machine, and that it is more suitable as a bomb-carrier than as a fighter.

I went through my examinations in Döberitz together with a dear fellow, Ober-Lieutenant von Lyncker. We got on very well with one another, had the same inclinations and the same ideas as to our future activity. Our aim was to fly Fokkers and to be included in a Fighting Squadron on the Western frontier. A year later we succeeded in working together for a short time. A fatal bullet hit my dear friend when bringing down his third aeroplane.

We had often passed merry hours in Döberitz. For instance, one of the things which we had to do was to land in strange country. I used the opportunity to combine the necessary with the agreeable. My favourable landing place outside of our aerodrome was the Buchow Estate, where I was well known. I was there invited to shoot wild pigs. The matter could be combined only with difficulty with duty, for on fine evenings I wished both to fly and to shoot pigs.

*Possibly a very early example of a Riesenflugzeug type, which is the next bigger thing than the Grossflugzeug type, which includes the Gothas, A.E.G.'s, Friedrichshafens, and other of the twin-engined types.

So I arranged for a place of landing in the neighbourhood of Buchow, whence I could easily reach my friends.

I took with me a second pilot who came as a passenger and sent him back in the evening. During the night I shot pigs and on the next morning was fetched by my pilot.

If I had not been fetched with the aeroplane I would have been in a hole, for I should have had to march on foot a distance of about six miles. So I required a man who would fetch me in any weather. It is not easy to find a man who will fetch you under any circumstances.

Once, when I had passed the night trying to shoot pigs, a tremendous snowfall set in. One could not see fifty yards ahead. My pilot was to fetch me at eight sharp. I hoped that for once he would not come. But suddenly I heard a humming noise – one could not see a thing – and five minutes later my beloved bird was squatting before me on the ground. Unfortunately some of his bones had been bent.

I BECOME A PILOT

On Christmas Day, 1915, I passed my third examination. In connection with it I flew to Schwerin, where the Fokker works are situated, and had a look at them. As passenger I took with me my mechanic, and from Schwerin I flew with him to Breslau, from Breslau to Schweidnitz, from thence to Lüben and then returned to Berlin. During my tour I landed in lots of different places in between, visiting relatives and friends. Being a trained observer, I did not find it difficult to find my way.

In March, 1916, I joined the Second Fighting Squadron before Verdun, and learned air fighting as a pilot. I learned how to handle a fighting aeroplane. I flew then a two-seater.

In the official communiqué of the 26th of April, 1916, I won a reference for the first time, although my name was not mentioned. Only my deeds appear in it. I had had built into my machine a machine-gun, which I had arranged very much in the way in which it is done in the Nieuport machines.* I was very proud of my idea. People laughed at the way I had fitted it up because the whole thing looked very primitive. Of course I swore by my new arrangement, and very soon I had an opportunity of ascertaining its practical value.

I encountered a hostile Nieuport machine which was apparently flown by a man who also was a beginner, for he acted extremely foolishly. When I flew towards him he flew away. Apparently he had trouble with his gun. I had not the idea to fight him, but thought: "What will happen if I now start shooting?" I flew after him, approached him as closely as possible, and then began firing a short series of well-aimed shots with my machine-gun. The Nieuport reared up in the air and turned over and over.

At first both my observer and I believe that this was one of the numerous tricks in which French fliers habitually indulge. However, his tricks did not cease. Turning over and over, the machine went lower and lower. At last my observer patted me on the head and called out to me: "I congratulate you. He is falling." As a matter of fact he fell into a forest behind Fort Douaumont and disappeared among the trees. It became clear to me that I had shot him down, but on the other side of the Front. I flew home and reported merely: "I had an aerial fight, and have shot down a Nieuport." The next day I read of my action in the official

*It is not clear whether this refers to a gun pointing upwards, as guns were at that time commonly fitted on the upper plane of the Nieuport, or whether the gun fired through the air-screw. Probably the latter fitting is meant. Later on one reads that he was then flying an Albatros, so it may have been a top gun.

communiqué. Of course I was very proud of my success but that Nieuport does not figure among the fifty-two aeroplanes which I have brought down.*

The communiqué of the 26th of April stated: "Two hostile flying machines have been shot down by aerial fighting above Fleury, south and west of Douaumont."

HOLCK'S DEATH

(30th of April, 1916.)

As a young pilot I once flew over Fort Douaumont at a moment when it was exposed to a violent drum-fire. I noticed that a German Fokker attacked three Caudron machines. I had the bad luck that a strong west wind was blowing. That was not favourable to me. The Fokker was driven over the town of Verdun in the course of the fight. I drew the attention of my observer to the struggle. He thought that the German fighting man must be a very smart fellow. We wondered whether it could be Boelcke, and intended to inquire when we came down. Then I saw to my horror that the German machine, which previously had attacked, had to fall back upon the defensive. The strength of the French fighting men had been increased to at least ten, and their combined assaults forced the German machine to go lower and lower. I could not fly to the German's aid. I was too far away from the battle. Besides, my heavy machine could not overcome the strong wind against me. The Fokker fought with despair. His opponents had rushed him down to an altitude of only about 1,800 feet. Suddenly, he was once more attacked by his opponents,

---

*Before writing the book, of course.

and he disappeared in a plunge in a small cloud. I breathed more easily, for, in my opinion, the cloud had saved him.

When I arrived at the aerodrome, I reported what I had seen, and was told that the Fokker man was Count Holck, my old comrade in the Eastern theatre of War.

Count Holck had dropped straight down, shot through the head. His death deeply affected me, for he was my model. I tried to imitate his energy, and he was a man among men also as a character.

I FLY IN A THUNDERSTORM

Our activity before Verdun was disturbed in the summer of 1916 by frequent thunderstorms. Nothing is more disagreeable for flying men than to have to go through a thunderstorm. For instance, on the Battle of the Somme a whole English flying squadron came down behind our lines, and became prisoners of war because they had been surprised by a thunderstorm.*

I had never yet made an attempt to get through thunder clouds, but I could not suppress my desire to make the experiment. During the whole day thunder was in the air. From my aerodrome at Mont I had flown over to the fortress of Metz near by in order to look after various things. During my return journey I had an adventure.

I was at the aerodrome of Metz, and intended to return to my own quarters. When I pulled my machine out of the hangar the first signs of an approaching thunderstorm

---

*Probably this means a patrol of one or two flights – of four machines each. One does not recall a whole squadron disappearing at once, though one or two squadrons had their whole personnel renewed one or two at a time in the course of a month or so.

became noticeable. Clouds which looked like a gigantic pitch-black wall approached from the north. Old experienced pilots urged me not to fly. However, I had promised to return, and I should have considered myself a coward if I had failed to come back because of a silly thunderstorm. Therefore I meant to try. When I started the rain began falling. I had to throw away my goggles, otherwise I should not have seen anything. The trouble was that I had to travel over the mountains of the Moselle, where the thunderstorm was just raging. I said to myself that probably I should be lucky and get through, and approached rapidly the black cloud which reached down to the earth. I flew at the lowest possible altitude. I was compelled absolutely to leap over houses and trees with my machine. Very soon I knew no longer where I was. The gale seized my machine as if it were a piece of paper, and drove it along. My heart sank within me. I could not land among the hills. I was therefore compelled to go on.

I was surrounded by an inky blackness. Beneath me the trees bent down in the gale. Suddenly I saw right in front of me a wooded height. I could not avoid it. My dear Albatros managed to take it. I was only able to fly in a straight line. Therefore I had to take every obstacle that I encountered. My flight became a jumping competition pure and simple. I had to jump over trees, villages, spires and steeples, for I had to keep within five yards of the ground. Otherwise I should have seen nothing at all. The lightning was playing around me. At that time I did not yet know that lightning cannot touch flying machines. I felt certain of my death, for it seemed to me inevitable that the gale would throw me at any moment into a village or a forest. Had the motor stopped working I should have been done for.

Then I saw that on the horizon the darkness became less thick. Over there the thunderstorm had passed. I would be

83

saved if I were able to get so far. Concentrating all my energy I steered towards the light.

Suddenly I had got out of the thunder-cloud. The rain was still falling in torrents. Still, I felt saved.

In pouring rain I landed on my aerodrome. Everyone was waiting for me, for Metz had reported my start, and had told them that I had been swallowed up by a thunder-cloud.

I shall never again fly through a thunderstorm unless the Fatherland should demand this.

When I look back all was very splendid. Notwithstanding the danger, I experienced during my flight glorious moments which I would not care to have missed.

MY FIRST TIME IN A FOKKER

From the beginning of my career as a pilot I had only a single ambition, the ambition to fly in a single-seater fighting machine. After worrying my commander for a long time I at last obtained permission to mount a Fokker. The revolving motor was a novelty to me. Besides, it was a strange feeling to be quite alone during the flight.

The Fokker belonged jointly to a friend of mine, who has died long ago and to myself. I flew in the morning, and he in the afternoon. Both he and I were afraid that the other fellow would smash the box. On the second day we flew towards the enemy. When I flew in the morning no Frenchman was to be seen. In the afternoon it was his turn. He started, but did not return. There was no news from him.

Late in the evening the infantry reported an aerial battle between a Nieuport and a German Fokker, in the course of which the German machine had apparently landed at the Mort Homme. Evidently the occupant was friend Reimann, for all the other flying men had returned. We regretted the fate of our brave comrade. In the middle of the night we heard over the telephone that a German flying officer had made unexpectedly an appearance in the front trenches at the Mort Homme. It appeared that this was Reimann. His motor had been smashed by a shot. He had been forced to land. As he was not able to reach our own lines he had come to the ground in No Man's Land. He had rapidly set fire to the machine, and had then quickly hidden himself in a mine crater. During the night he had slunk into our trenches. Thus ended our joint enterprise with a Fokker.

A few days later I was given another Fokker. This time I felt under a moral obligation to attend myself to its destruction. I was flying for the third time. When starting, the motor suddenly stopped working. I had to land right away in a field, and in a moment the beautiful machine was converted into a mass of scrap metal. It was a miracle that I was not hurt.

BOMBING IN RUSSIA

In June we were suddenly ordered to entrain. No one knew whither we were going, but we had the right idea, and we were not over-much surprised when our commander told us that we were going to Russia. We had travelled through the whole of Germany with our perambulating hotel, which consisted of dining and sleeping cars, and arrived at last at Kovel. There we remained in our railway cars. There are

85

many advantages in dwelling in a train. One is always ready to travel and need not change one's quarters.*

In the heat of the Russian summer a sleeping car is the most horrible instrument of martyrdom imaginable. Therefore, I agreed with some friends of mine, Gerstenberg and Scheele, to take quarters in the forest near by. We erected a tent and lived like gypsies. We had a lovely time.

In Russia our fighting squadron did a great deal of bomb throwing. Our occupation consisted in annoying the Russians. We dropped our eggs on their finest railway establishments. One day our whole squadron went out to bomb a very important railway station. The place was called Manjewicze, and was situated about twenty miles behind the Front. That was not very far. The Russians had planned an attack, and the station was absolutely crammed with colossal trains. Trains stood close to one another. Miles of rails were covered with them. One could easily see that from above. There was an object for bombing that was worth while.

One can become enthusiastic for anything. For a time I enthused about bomb throwing. It gave me a tremendous pleasure to bomb those fellows from above. Frequently I took part in two expeditions on a single day.

On the day mentioned our object was Manjewicze. Everything was ready. The aeroplanes were ready for starting. Every pilot tried his motor, for it is a painful thing to be forced to land against one's will on the wrong side of the front line, especially in Russia. The Russians hate the fliers. If they catch a flying man they will certainly kill him. That is the only risk one runs in Russia, for the Russians have no

*This is the first reference to the regular "travelling circus" idea, in which the whole squadron works as a self-contained unit, in a special train which moves its material, stores, spares, and mechanics, from place to place, and also provides living accommodation for the pilots.

aviators, or practically none. If a Russian flying man turns up, he is sure to have bad luck and will be shot down. The anti-aircraft guns used by Russia are sometimes quite good, but they are too few in number. Compared with flying in the West, flying in the East is absolutely a holiday.

The aëroplanes rolled heavily to the starting point. They carried bombs to the very limit of their capacity. Sometimes I lifted 3 cwts. of bombs with a normal C-type machine.* Besides, I had with me a very heavy observer who apparently had not suffered in any way from the food scarcity.† I had also with me a couple of machine-guns. I have never been able to make proper use of them in Russia. It is a pity that my collection of trophies contains not a single Russian.

Flying with a heavy machine which is carrying a great dead weight is no fun, especially during the mid-day summer heat in Russia. The barges sway in a very disagreeable manner. Of course, heavily laden though they are, they do not fall. The 150 h.p. prevent it.** At the same time it is no pleasant sensation to carry such a large quantity of explosives and petrol.

At last we got into a quiet atmosphere. Now came the enjoyment of bombing. It is very nice to be able to fly in a straight line and to have a definite object and definite orders. After having thrown one's bombs one has the feeling

*The German C-type machines are the two-seater reconnaissance types. The D-type are the single-seater fighters or "chaser" machines. The G-type are the big three-seater bombers.

†It is interesting to find a German joking about food scarcity in 1916 exactly as people in England joke about it in 1918. One is able thus to form some idea of the comparative states of the two countries, and to judge how Germany would have fared if the British blockade had been rigidly enforced at the beginning of the war.

**It was 150 horse-power in 1916. By the beginning of 1918 all modern German C-type machines had 260 h.p., and by April 1918 German biplanes with 500 h.p., in one engine, were beginning to appear. In consequence the extreme height (or "ceiling") of a C-type machine had risen from 12,000 feet to 20,000 feet.

that one has achieved something, while frequently, after searching for an enemy to give battle to, one comes home with a sense of failure, not having brought a hostile machine to the ground. Then one is apt to say to one's self: You have acted stupidly. It gave me a good deal of pleasure to throw bombs. After a while my observer learned how to fly perpendicularly over the objects to be bombed and to make use of the right moment for laying his egg with the assistance of his aiming telescope. The run to Manjewicze is very nice, and I have made it repeatedly.

We passed over gigantic forests which are probably inhabited by elks and lynxes. But the villages looked miserable. The only substantial village in the whole neighbourhood was Manjewicze. It was surrounded by innumerable tents, and countless barracks had been run up near the railway station. We could not make out the Red Cross. Before us another flying squadron had visited the place. That could be seen by smoking houses and barracks. They had not done badly. The exit of the station had obviously been blocked by a lucky hit. The engine was still steaming. The engine driver had probably dived into a shelter. On the other side of the station an engine was just coming out. Of course I felt tempted to hit it. We flew towards the engine and dropped a bomb a few hundred yards in front of it. We had the desired result. The engine stopped. We turned and continued throwing bomb after bomb on the station, carefully taking aim through our aiming telescope. We had plenty of time, for nobody interfered with us. It is true that an enemy aerodrome was quite in the neighbourhood, but there was no trace of hostile pilots. A few anti-aircraft guns were busy, but they shot not in our direction, but in another one. We reserved a bomb, hoping to make particularly good use of it on our way home.

Suddenly we noticed an enemy flying machine starting

from its hangar. The question was whether it would attack us. I did not believe in an attack. It was more likely that the flying man would seek security in the air, for when bombing machines are about the air is the safest place. We went home by roundabout ways, and looked for camps. It was particularly amusing to pepper the gentlemen down below with machine-guns. Half-savage tribes from Asia are much more startled when fired at from above than are educated Englishmen. It is particularly interesting to shoot at hostile cavalry. An aerial attack upsets them completely. Suddenly the lot of them rush away in all directions of the compass. I should not like to be the commander of a squadron of Cossacks which had been fired at with machine-guns from aeroplanes.*

By-and-bye we could recognise the German lines. We had to dispose of our last bomb, and we resolved to make a present of it to a Russian observation balloon – the only observation balloon they possessed. We could quite comfortably descend to within a few hundred yards of the ground in order to attack it. At first they began to haul it in very rapidly. When the bomb had been dropped the hauling stopped. I did not believe that I had hit it. I rather imagined that the Russians had left their chief in the air in the lurch and had run away. At last we reached our front and our trenches, and were surprised to find when we got home that we had been shot at from below. At least one of the planes had a hole in it.

Another time, and in the same neighbourhood, we were

---

*Attacks on troops on roads by low-flying aeroplanes were not regularly organised acts of war in those days, though such attacks had been made by R.N.A.S. pilots in Belgium in 1914. It is curious that despite the observed effects of the R.N.A.S. attacks, and the experiences of such men as von Richthofen, neither the British nor the German aeronautical authorities ever took the trouble to devote attention to this new method of war. The racial similarity of the two belligerents is marked in this as in other matters.

to meet an attack of the Russians who intended to cross the river Stokhod. We came to the danger spot laden with bombs and carrying a large number of cartridges for our machine-guns. On arrival at the Stokhod we were surprised to see that hostile cavalry was already crossing. They were passing over a single bridge. Immediately it was clear to us that one might do a tremendous lot of harm to the enemy by hitting the bridge.

Dense masses of men were crossing. We went as low as possible, and could clearly see that hostile cavalry were crossing with great rapidity. The first bomb fell near the bridge. The second and third followed immediately. They created a tremendous disorder. The bridge had not been hit. Nevertheless traffic across it had completely ceased. Men and animals were rushing away in all directions. We had thrown only three bombs, but the success had been excellent. Besides, a whole squadron of aeroplanes was following us. Lastly, we could do other things. My observer fired energetically into the crowd down below with his machine-gun, and we enjoyed it tremendously. Of course, I cannot say what real success we had. The Russians have not told us. Still I imagined that I alone had caused the Russian attack to fail. Perhaps the official account of the Russian War Office will give me details after the war.

AT LAST!

The August sun was almost unbearably hot on the sandy flying ground at Kovel. While we were chatting among ourselves one of my comrades said: "To-day the great Boelcke is coming on a visit to us, or rather to his brother!" In the evening the great man duly arrived. He was vastly admired by all, and he told us many interesting things about his journey to Turkey. He was just returning from Turkey, and was on the way to Headquarters. He imagined that he would go to the Somme to continue his work. He was to organise a fighting squadron. He was empowered to select from the Flying Service those men who seemed to him particularly qualified for his purpose.

I did not dare to ask him to be taken on. I did not feel bored by the fighting in Russia. On the contrary, we made extensive and interesting flights. We bombed the Russians at their stations. Still, the idea of fighting again on the Western Front attracted me. There is nothing finer for a young cavalry officer than the chase in the air.

The next morning Boelcke was to leave us. Quite early somebody knocked at my door, and before me stood the great man with the "Ordre pour le Mérite." I knew him, as I have previously mentioned, but still I had never imagined that he came to look me up in order to ask me to become his pupil. I almost fell on his neck when he inquired whether I cared to go with him to the Somme.

Three days later I sat in the railway train and travelled through the whole of Germany straight away to the new field of my activity. At last my greatest wish was fulfilled. From now onwards began the finest time of my life.

At that time I did not dare to hope that I should be as successful as I have been. When I left my quarters in the East a good friend of mine called out after me: "See that you do not come back without the 'Ordre pour le Mérite.'"

IV

MY FIRST ENGLISH VICTIM

*(17th September, 1916.)**

WE were at the butts trying our machine-guns. On the previous day we had received our new aeroplanes, and the next morning Boelcke was to fly with us. We all were beginners. None of us had had a success so far. Consequently everything that Boelcke told us was to us gospel truth. During the last few days he had, as he said, shot for breakfast every day one or two Englishmen.

The next morning, the 17th of September, was a gloriously fine day. It was therefore only to be expected that the English would be very active. Before we started Boelcke repeated to us his instructions, and for the first time we flew as a squadron commanded by the great man whom we followed blindly.

We had just arrived at the Front when we recognised a hostile flying squadron that was proceeding in the direction of Cambrai. Boelcke was of course the first to see it, for he saw a great deal more than ordinary mortals. Soon we understood the position, and everyone of us strove to follow Boelcke closely. It was clear to all of us that we should pass our first examination under the eyes of our beloved leader.

We approached slowly the hostile squadron. It could not

*This locates almost exactly the date of the formation of the first Bölcke Jagdstaffel of the "Circus" type.

92

escape us. We had intercepted it, for we were between the Front and the opponents. If they wished to go back they had to pass us. We counted the hostile machines. They were seven in number. We were only five. All the Englishmen flew large bomb-carrying two-seaters. In a few seconds the dance would begin.

Boelcke had come very near the first English machine, but he did not yet shoot. I followed. Close to me were my comrades. The Englishman nearest to me was travelling in a large machine painted in dark colours. I did not reflect very long, but took my aim and shot. He also fired and so did I, and both of us missed our aim. A struggle began, and the great point for me was to get to the rear of the fellow because I could only shoot forward with my gun. He was differently placed, for his machine-gun was moveable. It could fire in all directions.

Apparently he was no beginner, for he knew exactly that his last hour had arrived at the moment if I got at the back of him. At that time I had not yet the conviction ''He must fall'' which I have now on such occasions, but, on the contrary. I was curious to see whether he would fall. There is a great difference between the two feelings. When one has shot down one's first, second or third opponent, then one begins to find out how the trick is done.

My Englishman twisted and turned, flying in zig-zags. I did not think for a moment that the hostile squadron contained other Englishmen who conceivably might come to the aid of their comrades. I was animated by a single thought: ''The man in front of me must come down, whatever happens.'' At last a favourable moment arrived. My opponent had apparently lost sight of me. Instead of twisting and turning he flew straight along.* In a fraction of a second I was at his back with my excellent machine. I gave a

*Evidently a case of getting under the blind spot of the British machine.

93

THE RED AIR FIGHTER

short burst of shots with my machine-gun. I had gone so close that I was afraid I might dash into the Englishman. Suddenly I nearly yelled with joy, for the propeller of the enemy machine had stopped turning. Hurrah! I had shot his engine to pieces; the enemy was compelled to land, for it was impossible for him to reach his own lines. The English machine was swinging curiously to and fro. Probably something had happened to the pilot. The observer was no longer visible. His machine-gun was apparently deserted. Obviously I had hit the observer, and he had fallen from his seat.

The Englishman landed close to the flying ground of one of our squadrons. I was so excited that I landed also, and my eagerness was so great that I nearly smashed up my machine. The English flying machine and my own stood close together. I rushed to the English machine and saw that a lot of soldiers were running towards my enemy. When I arrived I discovered that my assumption had been correct. I had shot the engine to pieces, and both the pilot and observer were severely wounded. The observer died at once, and the pilot while being transported to the nearest dressing station. I honoured the fallen enemy by placing a stone on his beautiful grave.

When I came home Boelcke and my other comrades were already at breakfast. They were surprised that I had not turned up. I reported proudly that I had shot down an Englishman. All were full of joy, for I was not the only victor. Boelcke had shot down an opponent for breakfast as usual, and every one of the other men also had downed an enemy for the first time.

I would mention that since that time no English squadron ventured as far as Cambrai as long as Boelcke's squadron was there.*

*Cambrai at that time was a long way behind the front, and Bapaume was a more important mark for the British squadrons. So it may not have been worth while for squadrons to go so far afield as Cambrai. Single machines on long reconnaissance visited Cambrai regularly.

THE BATTLE OF THE SOMME

During my whole life I have not found a happier hunting ground that in the course of the Somme Battle. In the morning, as soon as I had got up, the first Englishmen arrived, and the last disappeared only long after sunset. Boelcke once said that this was the El Dorado of the flying men.

There was a time when Boelcke's bag of machines increased within two months from twenty to forty. We beginners had, at that time, not yet the experience of our master, and we were quite satisfied when we did not get a hiding. It was a beautiful time. Every time we went up we had a fight. Frequently we fought really big battles in the air. There were then from forty to sixty English machines, but unfortunately the Germans were often in the minority. With them quality was more important than quantity.

Still the Englishman is a smart fellow. That we must allow. Sometimes the English came down to a very low altitude and visited Boelcke in his quarters, upon which they threw their bombs. They absolutely challenged us to battle, and never refused fighting. On the other hand the French take the greatest trouble to avoid meeting their opponents in the air.*

We had a delightful time with our chasing squadron. The spirit of our leader animated all his pupils. We trusted him blindly. There was no possibility that one of us would be left behind. Such a thought was incomprehensible to us. Animated by that spirit we gaily diminished the number of our enemies.

On the day when Boelcke fell the squadron had brought

*At this period the French Service d'Aviation was in rather a bad way as regards the quality and quantity of its aeroplanes so that possibly this remark was justifiable at the time. At the beginning of 1918 things were very different.

95

down forty opponents. By now the number has been increased by more than a hundred. Boelcke's spirit lives still among his capable successors.

BOELCKE'S DEATH

(28th October, 1916.)

One day we were flying, once more led by Boelcke against the enemy. We had always a wonderful feeling of security when he was with us. After all he was the one and only. The weather was very gusty, and there were many clouds. There were no aeroplanes about except fighting machines.

From a long distance we saw two impertinent English-men in the air, who also seemed to enjoy the rotten weather. We were six, and they were two. If they had been twenty, and if Boelcke had given us the signal to attack, we should not have been at all surprised.

The struggle began in the usual way. Boelcke tackled the one and I the other. I had to let go because one of the German machines got in my way. I looked around and noticed Boelcke settling his victim about two hundred yards away from me.

It was the usual thing. Boelcke shot down his opponent and I had to look on. Close to Boelcke flew a good friend of his. It was an interesting struggle. Both men were shooting. It was likely that the Englishman would fall at any moment. Suddenly I noticed an unnatural movement of the two German flying machines. Immediately I thought: "Collision." I had not yet seen a collision in the air. I had imagined that it would look quite different. In reality, what happened was not a collision. The two machines merely touched one another. However, if two machines go at the

1. Manfred von Richthofen. (NH)

2. Von Richthofen's commander and mentor, Oswald Boelcke, seated in a Jasta 2 Albatros DI, late 1916. (CB)

3. Von Richthofen (with scarf and cavalry spurs) shortly after taking command of Jasta 11 in January 1917. The two aircraft are the Albatros DIII (left) and the Halberstadt DII. The pilot on the right is Leutnant Alfred Gerstenberg. (CB)

4. Oswald Boelcke prior to his award of the Pour Le Mérite. (NH)

5. Albatros DII flown by Leutnant Max Böhme of Jasta 5 when he was captured in March 1917. Böhme had previously served in Jasta 2. (CB)

7. Leutnant Kurt Wolff and von Richthofen in Belgium. Wolff was killed in action in September 1917 following 33 victories. (NH)

6. Von Richthofen seated in the cockpit of his Albatros Scout, 1917. (CB)

8. Line up of Jasta 11 on Douai airfield in April 1917. Richthofen's aircraft, Albatros DIII 2253/17 – all red – second from the front. (NH)

9. General Ludendorff inspecting Jasta 11 at Marcke, Belgium, on 19th August 1917. Richthofen's Red Albatros, D2059/17, stands waiting. (CB)

10. Von Richthofen recovering from his head wound received on 6th July 1917. With him is Wilhelm Reinhard (20 victories) who commanded JGI after Manfred's death. (NH)

11. Oblt Eduard Dostler, leader of Jasta 6, upon his award in August 1917 of the Pour Le Mérite. Von Richthofen has put his own 'Blue Max' round Dostler's neck in celebration. (NH)

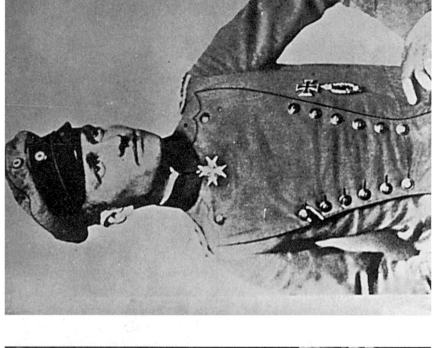

13. The well known portrait of Manfred von Richthofen, with his Pour Le Mérite, Iron Cross 1st and 2nd class and pilot's badge. (NH)

12. Von Richthofen, the Red Air Fighter. (NH)

14. Manfred with his Albatros CIX, which he used for his personal transport. Note airman helping him to put on his flying overalls while another waits with his helmet and goggles. (CB)

15. Manfred's brother, Lothar von Richthofen, being helped down from his Jasta 11 Albatros Scout, 1917. (CB)

17. Manfred (far right) with Kurt Wolff, an Austrian officer, and Ltn Krefft, Jasta 11's Technical officer. (NH)

16. Manfred with Oberstleutnant Hermann Thomsen, commander of the German Air Service staff and General von Hoeppner, Officer Commanding the Air Service. (CB)

18. Major Albrecht von Richthofen and his two sons, Manfred (left) and Lothar, who between them brought down 120 Allied aircraft. (NH)

19. The arrival of the Fokker FI Triplane to Jasta 11. This machine, 102/17, became Manfred's personal aircraft for a time. Anthony Fokker is seated in the Triplane, talking to General von Lossberg. Leutnant Hans Adam (21 victories) far right. (CB)

20. Lothar von Richthofen received his Pour Le Mérite in 1917 and commanded Jasta 11 after his brother took charge of JGI. (NH)

21. JGI Staffelführers in March 1918: l to r: Kurt Wüsthoff Jasta 4 (27 victories); Willy Reinhard, Jasta 11 (20 victories); von Richthofen; Erich Löwenhardt, Jasta 10 (53 victories); Lothar von Richthofen, Jasta 11 (40 victories). (CB)

22. Von Richthofen talking to his 'Circus' pilots in 1918, over a Fokker Triplane. (CB)

23. Fokker Triplane 163/17 in the winter snow of 1917/18. (CB)

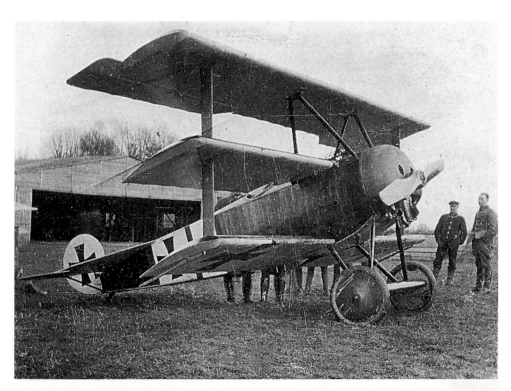

24. Jasta 11 Fokker Drl Triplane (163/17) flown by Leutnant von Linsingen. (CB)

25. Captain Roy Brown DSC & bar, 209 Squadron, who was in action with von Richthofen when he was killed, 21st April 1918. Brown died in 1944. (CB)

tremendous pace of flying machines, the slightest contact has the effect of a violent concussion.

Boelcke drew away from his victim and descended in large curves. I had not the feeling that he was falling, but when I saw him descending below me I noticed that part of his planes had broken off. I could not see what was happening afterwards, but in the clouds he lost an entire plane. Now his machine was no longer controllable. It fell accompanied all the time by Boelcke's faithful friend.

When we reached home we found already the report, "Boelcke is dead!" We could scarcely realise it.

The greatest pain was, of course, felt by the man who had the misfortune to be involved in the accident.

It is a strange thing that everybody who met Boelcke imagined that he alone was his true friend. I have made the acquaintance of about forty men, each of whom imagined that he alone had Boelcke's affection. Men whose names were unknown to Boelcke believed that he was particularly fond of them. This is a curious phenomenon which I have never noticed in anyone else. Boelcke had not a personal enemy. He was equally pleasant to everybody, making no differences.

The only one who was perhaps more intimate with him than the others was the very man who had the misfortune to be in the accident which caused his death.

Nothing happens without God's will. That is the only consolation which we can put to our soul during this war.

MY EIGHTH VICTIM

In Boelcke's time eight victims was quite a respectable number. Those who hear nowadays of the colossal bags made by certain aviators must feel convinced that it has become easier

97

to shoot down a machine. I can assure those who hold that opinion that the flying business is becoming more difficult from month to month, and even from week to week. Of course, with the increasing number of aeroplanes one gets increased opportunities for shooting down one's enemies, but, at the same time, the opportunity increases of being shot down one's-self. The armament of our enemies is steadily improving and their number is increasing.* When Immelmann shot down his first victim he had the good fortune to find an opponent who carried not even a machine gun. Such little innocents one finds nowadays only at the training ground for beginners.

On the 9th of November, 1916, I flew towards the enemy with my little comrade Immelmann,† who then was eighteen years old. We both were in Boelcke's squadron of chasing aeroplanes. We had previously met one another and had got on very well. Comradeship is a most important thing. We went to work. I had already bagged seven enemies and Immelmann five. At that time this was quite a lot.

Soon after our arrival over the lines we saw a squadron of bombing aeroplanes. They were coming along with impertinent assurance. They arrived in enormous numbers, as was usual during the Somme Battle. I think there were about forty or fifty machines approaching. I cannot give the exact number. They had selected an object for their bombs not far from our aerodrome. I reached them when they had almost attained their objective. I approached the last machine. My first few shots incapacitated the hostile machine gunner. Possibly they had tickled the pilot too. At

---

*This testimony to the improvement in the aerial equipment of the British Army is well worthy of note.

†This is evidently a junior Immelmann of Bölcke's squadron, and not the famous Immelmann, who was already dead before the Bölcke squadron came into existence.

any rate he resolved to land with his bombs. I fired a few more shots to accelerate his progress downwards. He fell close to our flying ground at Lagnicourt.

While I was fighting my opponent, Immelmann had tackled another Englishman and had brought him down in the same locality. Both of us flew quickly home in order to have a look at the machines we had downed. We jumped into a motor car, drove in the direction where our victims lay, and had to run a long distance through the fields. It was very hot. Therefore I unbuttoned all my garments, even the collar and the shirt. I took off my jacket, left my cap in the car, but took with me a big stick. My boots were muddy up to the knees. I looked like a tramp. I arrived in the vicinity of my victim. In the meantime a lot of people had of course gathered around.

At one spot there was a group of officers. I approached them, saluted them, and asked the first one whom I met whether he could tell me anything about the aspect of the aerial battle. It is always interesting to find out how a fight in the air looks to the people down below. I was told that the English machines had thrown bombs and that the aeroplane that had come down was still carrying its bombs.

The officer who gave me this information took my arm, went with me to the other officers, asked my name and introduced me to them. I did not like it, for my attire was rather disarranged. On the other hand, all the officers looked as spick and span as on parade. I was introduced to a personage who impressed me rather strangely. I noticed a General's trousers, an Order at the neck, an unusually youthful face and undefinable epaulettes. In short, the personage seemed extraordinary to me. During our conversation I buttoned my trousers and collar and adopted a somewhat military attitude.*

*One has heard stories uncommonly like this from R.F.C. officers.

I had no idea who the officer was. I took my leave and went home again. In the evening the telephone was ringing and I was told that the undefinable somebody with whom I had been talking had been His Royal Highness the Grand-Duke of Saxe-Coburg Gotha.

I was ordered to go to him. It was known that the English had intended to throw bombs on his headquarters. Apparently I had helped to keep the aggressors away from him. Therefore I was given the Saxe-Coburg-Gotha medal for bravery.

I always enjoy this adventure when I look at the medal.

MAJOR HAWKER

I was extremely proud when one fine day I was informed that the aviator whom I had brought down on the 23rd November, 1916, was the English Immelmann.

In view of the character of our fight it was clear to me that I had been tackling a flying champion.

One day I was blithely flying to give chase when I noticed three Englishmen who also had apparently gone a-hunting. I noticed that they were interested in my direction, and as I felt much inclination to have a fight I did not want to disappoint them.

I was flying at a lower altitude. Consequently I had to wait until one of my English friends tried to drop on me. After a short while he came sailing along and wanted to tackle me in the rear. After firing five shots he had to stop, for I had swerved in a sharp curve.

The Englishman tried to catch me up in the rear while I tried to get behind him. So we circled round and round like madmen after one another at an altitude of about 10,000 feet.

First we circled twenty times to the left, and then thirty times to the right. Each tried to get behind and above the other.

Soon I discovered that I was not meeting a beginner. He had not the slightest intention to break off the fight. He was travelling in a box* which turned beautifully. However, my packing case† was better at climbing than his. But I succeeded at last in getting above and beyond my English waltzing partner.

When we had got down to about 6,000 feet without having achieved anything particular, my opponent ought to have discovered that it was time for him to take his leave. The wind was favourable to me, for it drove us more and more towards the German position. At last we were above Bapaume, about half a mile behind the German front. The gallant fellow was full of pluck, and when we had got down to about 3,000 feet he merrily waved to me as if he would say, Well, how do you do?

The circles which we made around one another were so narrow that their diameter was probably no more than 250 or 300 feet. I had time to take a good look at my opponent. I looked down into his carriage and could see every movement of his head. If he had not had his cap on I would have noticed what kind of a face he was making.

My Englishman was a good sportsman, but by and by the thing became a little too hot for him. He had to decide whether he would land on German ground or whether he would fly back to the English lines. Of course he tried the latter, after having endeavoured in vain to escape me by

*Major Hawker was flying a de Havilland II with a 100 h.p. Monosoupape Gnôme engine, a species of "box-kite" single-seater biplane, albeit very fast and handy.

†Von Richthofen's Albatros biplane, having a wood-covered fuselage, would resemble a packing-case, so the German slang phrases are really rather apt.

loopings and such tricks. At that time his first bullets were flying around me, for so far neither of us had been able to do any shooting.

When he had come down to about 300 feet he tried to escape by flying in a zig-zag course, which makes it difficult for an observer on the ground to shoot. That was my most favourable moment. I followed him at an altitude of from 250 feet to 150 feet, firing all the time. The Englishman could not help falling. But the jamming of my gun nearly robbed me of my success.

My opponent fell shot through the head 150 feet behind our line. His machine gun was dug out of the ground and it ornaments the entrance of my dwelling.*

I GET THE "ORDRE POUR LE MERITE"

I had brought down my sixteenth victim, and I had come to the head of the list of all the flying chasers. I had obtained the aim which I had set myself. In the previous years I had said in fun to my friend Lyncke, when we were trained together, and when he asked me: "What is your object? What will you obtain by flying?" – "I would like to be the first of the chasers. That must be very nice." That I should succeed in this I did not believe myself. Other people also did not expect my success. Boelcke is supposed to have said,

*One gathers that this account is substantially accurate. The other two British machines who were with Major Hawker became involved with von Richthofen's four followers and with five other German chasers which came into the fight from a higher altitude. These two, after a busy time, fought their way out, while Major Hawker was fighting von Richthofen. The only flaw in the story is that in fact one of the upper German machines dived onto Major Hawker, who, apparently, in avoiding it, came into action with von Richthofen.

not to me personally, – I have only heard the report – when asked: "Which of the fellows is likely to become a good chaser?" – "That is the man!" pointing his finger in my direction.

Boelcke and Immelmann were given the Ordre Pour le Mérite when they had brought down their eighth aeroplane. I had downed twice that number. The question was, What would happen to me? I was very curious. It was rumoured that I was to be given command of a chasing squadron.

One fine day a telegram arrived which stated: "Lieutenant von Richthofen is appointed commander of the Eleventh Chasing Squadron."

I must say I was annoyed. I had learnt to work so well with my comrades of Boelcke's Squadron, and now I had to begin all over again working hand in hand with different people. It was a beastly nuisance. Besides I should have preferred the Ordre Pour le Mérite.

Two days later, when we were sitting sociably together, we men of the Boelcke's Squadron, celebrating my departure, a telegram from Headquarters arrived. It stated that His Majesty had graciously condescended to give me the Ordre Pour le Mérite. Of course my joy was tremendous. It was balm on my wound.

I had never imagined that it would be so delightful to command a chasing squadron. Even in my dreams I had not imagined that there would ever be a von Richthofen's squadron of aeroplanes.

"LE PETIT ROUGE"

It occurred to me to have my packing case painted all over in staring red. The result was that everyone got to know my red bird. My opponents also seemed to have heard of the colour transformation.

During a fight on quite a different section of the front I had the good fortune to shoot into a Vickers' two-seater which was peacefully photographing the German artillery position. My friend the photographer had not the time to defend himself. He had to make haste to get down upon firm ground, for his machine began to give suspicious indications of fire. When we notice that phenomenon, we say: "He stinks!" As it turned out, it was really so. When the machine was coming to earth it burst into flames.

I felt some human pity for my opponent and had resolved not to cause him to fall down but merely to compel him to land. I did so particularly because I had the impression that my opponent was wounded, for he did not fire a single shot.

When I had got down to an altitude of about 1,500 feet engine trouble compelled me to land without making any curves. The result was very comical. My enemy with his burning machine landed smoothly, while I, his conqueror, came down next to him in the barbed wire of our trenches and my machine overturned.*

The two Englishmen who were not a little surprised at my collapse, greeted me like sportsmen. As mentioned before, they had not fired a shot, and they could not understand why I had landed so clumsily. They were the first two Englishmen whom I had brought down alive. Consequently, it gave me particular pleasure to talk to them. I asked them whether they had previously seen my machine in the air, and one of them replied, "Oh, yes. I know your machine very well. We call it 'Le Petit Rouge.'"

*This incident confirms the impression that the small Albatros biplanes are difficult to land except in a properly prepared aerodrome.

ENGLISH AND FRENCH FLYING

(February, 1917.)

I was trying to compete with Boelcke's Squadron. Every evening we compared our bags. However, Boelcke's pupils are smart rascals. I cannot get ahead of them. The utmost one can do is to draw level with them. The Boelcke staffel has an advantage over my people of 100 aeroplanes downed. I must allow them to retain it. Everything depends on whether we have for opponents those French tricksters or those daring fellows the English. I prefer the English. Frequently the daring of the latter can only be described as stupidity. In their eyes it may be pluck and bravery.

The great thing in air fighting is that the decisive factor does not lie in trick flying but solely in the personal ability and energy of the aviator. A flying man may be able to loop and do all the tricks imaginable and yet he may not succeed in shooting down a single enemy. In my opinion the aggressive spirit is everything, and that spirit is very strong in us Germans. Hence we shall always retain the domination of the air.*

The French have a different character. They like to set traps and to attack their opponents unawares. That cannot easily be done in the air. Only a beginner can be caught, and one cannot set traps, because an aeroplane cannot hide itself. The invisible aeroplane has not yet been discovered. Sometimes, however, the Gallic blood asserts itself. Then Frenchmen will then attack. But the French attacking spirit is like bottled lemonade. It lacks tenacity.

*Except when faced by Britain pilots in approximately equal numbers and equally well mounted. It is interesting here to recall the dictum of General von Höppner, the chief of the German Flying Service, who said that the English are dangerous opponents and show by their fighting spirit that they are of Germanic race. It will be noticed that von Richthofen repeats the sentiment later on.

In Englishmen, on the other hand, one notices that they are of Germanic blood. Sportsmen easily take to flying, but Englishmen see in flying nothing but a sport. They take a perfect delight in looping the loop, flying on their back, and indulging in other tricks for the benefit of our soldiers in the trenches. All these tricks may impress people who attend a Sports Meeting, but the public at the battle-front is not as appreciative of these things. It demands higher qualifications than trick flying. Therefore, the blood of English pilots will have to flow in streams.

I AM SHOT DOWN

(Middle of March, 1917.)

I have had an experience which might perhaps be described as being shot down. At the same time, I call it being shot down only when one falls down. To-day I got into trouble, but I escaped with a whole skin.

I was flying with the squadron and noticed an opponent who also was flying in a squadron. It happened above the German artillery position in the neighbourhood of Lens. I had to fly quite a distance to get there. It tickles one's nerves to fly towards the enemy, especially when one can see him from a long distance and when several minutes must elapse before one can start fighting. I imagine that at such a moment my face turns a little pale, but unfortunately I have never had a mirror with me. I like that feeling, for it is a wonderful nerve stimulant.

One observes the enemy from afar. One has recognised that his squadron is really an enemy formation. One counts the number of the hostile machines and considers whether the conditions are favourable or unfavourable. A factor of enormous importance is whether the wind forces one away from our front or towards our front. For instance, I once shot down an Englishman. I fired the fatal shot above the English position. However, the wind was so strong that his machine came down close to the German kite-balloons.

We Germans had five machines. Our opponents were three times as numerous. The English flew about like midges. It is not easy to disperse a swarm of machines which fly together in good order. It is impossible for a single machine. It is extremely difficult for several aeroplanes, particularly if the difference in number is as great as it was in this case. However, one feels such a superiority over the enemy that one does not doubt for a moment of success.

The aggressive spirit, the offensive, is the chief thing everywhere in war, and the air is no exception.* However, the enemy had the same idea. I noticed that at once. As soon as they noticed us they turned round and attacked us. Now we five had to look sharp. If one of them should fall there might be a lot of trouble for all of us. We went closer together and allowed the foreign gentlemen to approach us.

I watched whether one of the fellows would hurriedly take leave of his colleagues. One of them was stupid enough to depart alone. I could reach him and I said to myself, "That man is lost!" Shouting aloud, I went after him. I came up to him, or at least was getting very near him. He started shooting prematurely, which showed that he was nervous. So I said to myself, "Go on shooting. You won't hit me." He shot with a kind of munition which ignites. So I could see his shots passing me. I felt as if I were sitting in front of a gigantic watering pot. The sensation was not pleasant. Still, the English usually shoot with this beastly

*The doctrine of Clausewitz and of the leading German military writers.

107

stuff, and so we must try and get accustomed to it.* One can get accustomed to anything. At the moment, I think, I laughed aloud. But soon I got a lesson. When I had approached the Englishman quite closely, when I had come to a distance of about 300 feet, I got ready for firing, aimed and gave a few trial shots. The machine-guns were in order. The decision would be there before long. In my mind's eye I saw my enemy dropping.

My former excitement was gone. In such a position one thinks quite calmly and collectedly and weighs the probabilities of hitting and of being hit. Altogether the fight itself is the least exciting part of the business as a rule. He who gets excited in fighting is sure to make mistakes. He will never get his enemy down. Besides calmness is, after all, a matter of habit. At any rate, in this case I did not make a mistake. I approached my man up to within fifty yards. I fired some well-aimed shots and thought that I was bound to be successful. That was my idea. But suddenly I heard a tremendous bang when I had scarcely fired ten cartridges, and presently again something hit my machine. It became clear to me that I had been hit, or rather my machine. At the same time I noticed a fearful stench of petrol, and I observed that the motor was running slack. The Englishman noticed it too, for he started shooting with redoubled energy, while I had to stop it.

I went right down. Instinctively I switched off the engine, and indeed it was high time to do this. When one's petrol tank has been holed and when the infernal liquid is squirting around one's legs the danger of fire is very great.

*The reference is to what are called ''tracer'' bullets. The hind end of the bullet contains a phosphorous mixture which leaves a trail of smoke and so indicates to the gunner where his bullets are going. If such a bullet penetrates a petrol tank or passes through escaping petrol – due to a perforated tank or a cut petrol-pipe – it sets the petrol on fire, but the prime reason is to trace the course of the shot. The Germans use similar bullets as largely as do the Allies.

108

One has in front an explosion engine of more than 150 h.p. which is red hot. If a single drop of petrol should fall on it the whole machine would be in flames.*

I left in the air a thin white cloud. I knew its meaning from my enemies. Its appearance is the first sign of a coming explosion. I was at an altitude of 9,000 feet, and had to travel a long distance to get down. By the kindness of Providence my engine stopped running. I have no idea with what rapidity I went downward. At any rate the speed was so great that I could not put my head out of the machine without being pressed back by the rush of air.

Soon I had lost sight of my enemy. I had only time to see what my four comrades were doing while I was dropping to the ground. They were still fighting. Their machine-guns and those of their opponents could be heard. Then I notice a rocket. Is it a signal of the enemy? No, it cannot be. The light is too great for a rocket. Evidently a machine is on fire. What machine? The burning machine looks exactly as if it were one of our own. No! Praise the Lord, it is one of the enemy's! Who can have shot him down? Immediately afterwards a second machine drops out and falls perpendicularly to the ground, turning, turning, turning exactly as I did, but suddenly it recovers its balance. It flies straight towards me. It also is an Albatros. No doubt it had the same experience as I had.

I had fallen to an altitude of perhaps 1,000 feet, and had to look out for a landing. Now, such a sudden landing usually leads to breakages, and these are occasionally serious. I found a meadow. It was not very large, but it just

---

*This is a mistaken idea, common to many pilots who are not motor engineers. Fire in such cases is caused by petrol or petrol vapour being set alight by a spark from the magneto, which because the air-screw is still revolving continues to generate sparks internally even when switched off. A merely red-hot pipe in an engine would not cause a petrol fire.

sufficed if I used due caution. Besides it was favourably situated on the high road near Hénin-Liétard. There I meant to land.

Everything went as desired, and my first thought was, "What has become of the other fellow?" He landed a few kilometres from the spot where I had come to the ground.

I had ample time to inspect the damage. My machine had been hit a number of times. The shot which caused me to give up the fight had gone through both the petrol tanks. I had not a drop of petrol left, and the engine itself also had been damaged by shots. It was a pity, for it had worked so well.

I let my legs dangle out of the machine, and probably made a very silly face. In a moment I was surrounded by a large crowd of soldiers. Then came an officer. He was quite out of breath. He was terribly excited. No doubt something fearful had happened to him. He rushed towards me, gasped for air and asked: "I hope that nothing has happened to you? I have followed the whole affair, and am terribly excited! Good Lord, it looked awful!" I assured him that I felt quite well, jumped down from the side of my machine and introduced myself to him. Of course he did not understand a particle of my name. However, he invited me to go in his motor car to Hénin-Liétard, where he was quartered. He was an Engineer Officer.

We were sitting in the motor and were commencing our ride. My host was still extraordinarily excited. He jumped up, and asked: "Good Lord, but where is your chauffeur?" At first I did not quite understand what he meant. Probably I looked puzzled. Then it dawned upon me that he thought that I was the observer of a two-seater, and that he asked after the fate of my pilot. I pulled myself together, and said in the driest tones: "I always drive myself." Of course the word "drive" is absolutely taboo among the flying men.

An aviator does not drive, he flies. In the eyes of the kind gentleman I had obviously lost caste when he discovered that I "drove" my own aeroplane. The conversation began to slacken.

We arrived at his quarters. I was still dressed in my dirty and oily leather jacket, and had round my neck a thick wrap. On our journey he had of course asked me a tremendous number of questions. Altogether he was far more excited than I was.

When we got to his diggings he forced me to lie down on the sofa, or at least he tried to force me, because, he argued, I was bound to be terribly done up through my fight. I assured him that this was not my first aerial battle, but he did not, apparently, give me much credence. Probably I did not look very martial.

After we had been talking for some time he asked me of course the celebrated question: "Have you ever brought down a machine?" As I said before he had probably not understood my name. So I answered nonchalantly, "Oh, yes. I have done so now and then." He replied: "Indeed! Perhaps you have shot down two?" I answered: "No. Not two, but twenty-four." He smiled, repeated his question and gave me to understand that, when he was speaking about shooting down an aeroplane, he meant not shooting *at* an aeroplane, but shooting *into* an aeroplane in such a manner that it would fall to the ground and remain there. I immediately assured him that I entirely shared his conception of the meaning of the words "shooting down."

Now I had completely lost caste with him. He was convinced that I was a fearful liar. He left me sitting where I was, and told me that a meal would be served in an hour. If I liked I could join in. I accepted his invitation, and slept soundly for an hour. Then we went to the Officer's Club. Arrived at the Club I was glad to find that I was wearing the Ordre pour le Mérite.

111

Unfortunately I had no uniform jacket underneath my greasy leather coat, but only a waistcoat. I apologised for being so badly dressed. Suddenly my good officer discovered on me the Ordre pour le Mérite. He was speechless with surprise, and assured me that he did not know my name. I gave him my name once more. Now it seemed to dawn upon him that he had heard my name before. He feasted me with oysters and champagne, and I did gloriously until at last my orderly arrived and fetched me with my car.*

I learned from him before leaving his quarters that comrade Lübbert had once more justified his nick-name. He was generally called "the bullet-catcher," for his machine suffered badly in every fight. Once it was hit sixty-four times. Yet he had not been wounded. This time he had received a glancing shot on the chest, and he was by this time in hospital. I flew his machine to port. Unfortunately this excellent officer, who promised to become another Boelcke, died a few weeks later a hero's death for the Fatherland.

In the evening I could assure my kind host of Hénin-Liétard that I had increased my "bag" to twenty-five.

*This is another of those touches of nature which make all aviators akin. It might equally well have been told by many a British officer, so far as the incredulousness of the Sapper is concerned. Probably, however, oysters and champagne were not so easily found behind the British Front, except perhaps in certain chosen spots in Amiens, such as that to which "Contact" refers in his description of a pleasant evening there "with two charming ladies and the widow Cliquot."

V

A FLYING-MAN'S ADVENTURE

(End of March, 1917.)

THE name "Siegfried position" is probably known to every young man in Germany. During the time when we withdrew towards the Siegfried Line the activity in the air was of course very great. We allowed our enemies to occupy the territory which we had evacuated, but we did not allow them to occupy the air as well. The chaser squadron which Boelcke had trained looked after the English flying men. The English had hitherto fought a war of position on the ground, and they ventured to abandon it for a war of movement only with the utmost caution.

That was the time when our dear Prince Friedrich Karl gave his life for the Fatherland.

In the course of a hunting expedition of the Boelcke chaser squadron, Lieutenant Voss* had defeated an Englishman in

---

*Voss was afterwards shot in a fight by the late Lieut. Rhys-Davids, D.S.O., M.C. In this fight, which is said to have been one of the most gallant actions in the war, Voss was flying a Fokker triplane with a French le Rhône engine, taken out of a captured machine. He was attacked by six British S.E.'s, all faster than he was. His solitary companion, on an Albatros, was shot down at the first onset, but Voss, instead of getting away, as he could have done, stayed and fought the crowd. His manœuvring and shooting are said to have been wonderful. Every British machine was hit, but none was brought down, and Voss himself finally fell to a direct attack by Mr. Rhys-Davids.

113

an aerial duel. He was forced to go down to the ground, and landed in neutral territory between the lines, in No Man's Land. In this particular case we had abandoned a stretch of territory, but the enemy had not yet occupied it. Only English and German patrols were about in the unoccupied zone. The English flying machine was standing between the two lines. Our good Englishman probably believed that the ground was already in English possession, and he was justified in thinking so.

Lieutenant Voss was of a different opinion. Without a moment's hesitation he landed close to his victim. With great rapidity he transferred the Englishman's machine-guns and other useful things to his own aeroplane, lit a match and in a few minutes the English machine stood in flames. Then he waved smilingly from his victorious aeroplane to the English who were rushing along from all sides, and was off.

MY FIRST DOUBLE EVENT

The 2nd April, 1917, was a very warm day for my squadron.* From my quarters I could clearly hear the drum-fire of the guns, which was again particularly violent.

I was still in bed when my orderly rushed into the room and exclaimed: "Sir, the English are here!" Sleepy as I was I looked out of the window, and really there were my dear friends circling over the flying ground. I jumped out of my bed, and into my clothes in a jiffy. My Red Bird had been pulled out, and was ready for starting. My mechanics knew

---

*It was reported in the British G.H.Q. Communiqué on this day that six of our machines were missing.

114

that I should probably not allow such a favourable moment to go by unused. Everything was ready. I snatched up my furs, and then went off.

I was the last to start. My comrades were much nearer to the enemy. I feared that my prey would escape me, that I should have to look on from a distance while the others were fighting. Suddenly one of the impertinent fellows tried to drop down upon me. I allowed him to come near, and then we started a merry quadrille. Sometimes my opponent flew on his back and sometimes he did other tricks. He had a two-seater fighter. I was his master, and very soon I recognised that he could not escape me.

During an interval in the fighting I convinced myself that we were alone. It followed that the victory would belong to him who was calmest, who shot best and who had the clearest brain in a moment of danger. After a short time I had got him beneath me without having seriously hurt him with my gun. We were at least two kilometres from the front. I thought he intended to land, but there I had made a mistake. Suddenly, when he was only a few yards above the ground, I noticed how he once more went off on a straight course. He tried to escape me. That was too bad. I attacked him again, and I went so low that I feared to touch the roofs of the houses of the village beneath me. The Englishman defended himself up to the last moment. At the very end I felt that my engine had been hit. Still I did not let go. He had to fall. He rushed at full speed right into a block of houses.

There was little left to be done. This was once more a case of splendid daring. He defended himself to the last. However, in my opinion he showed after all more stupid fool-hardiness than courage. This was again one of the cases where one must differentiate between energy and idiocy. He had to come down in any case, but he paid for his stupidity with his life.

I was delighted with the performance of my red machine during its morning work, and returned to our quarters. My comrades were still in the air and they were very surprised, when we met at breakfast, when I told them that I had scored my thirty-second machine.

A very young Lieutenant had "bagged" his first aeroplane. We were all very merry and prepared everything for further battles.

I then went and groomed myself. I had not had time to do it previously. I was visited by a dear friend, Lieutenant Voss of Boelcke's Squadron. We chatted. Voss had downed on the previous day his twenty-third machine. He was next to me on the list, and is at present my most redoubtable competitor.

When he wanted to fly home I intended to accompany him part of the way. We went on a round-about way over the fronts. The weather had turned so bad that we could not hope to find any more game.

Beneath us there were dense clouds. Voss did not know the country, and he began to feel uncomfortable. When we passed above Arras I met my brother, who also is in my squadron, and who had lost it. He joined us. Of course he recognised me at once by the colour of my machine.

Suddenly we saw a patrol approaching from the other side. Immediately the thought occurred to me: "Now comes number thirty-three." Although there were nine Englishmen and although they were on their own territory they preferred to avoid battle. I thought that perhaps it would be better for me to repaint my machine. Nevertheless we caught them up. The important thing in aeroplanes is that they shall be speedy.

I was nearest to the enemy, and attacked the man to the rear. To my greatest delight I noticed that he accepted battle, and my pleasure was increased when I discovered that his comrades deserted him. So I had once more a single fight.

It was a fight similar to the one which I had had in the morning. My opponent did not make matters easy for me. He knew the fighting business, and it was particularly awkward for me that he was a good shot. To my great regret that was quite clear to me.

A favourable wind came to my aid. It drove both of us into the German lines.* My opponent discovered that the matter was not as simple as he had imagined. So he plunged, and disappeared in a cloud. He had nearly saved himself.

I plunged after him and dropped out of the cloud and, as luck would have it, found myself close behind him. I fired and he fired without any tangible result. At last I hit him. I noticed a ribbon of white petrol vapour. He must land, for his engine had come to a stop.

He was a stubborn fellow. He was bound to recognise that he had lost the game. If he continued shooting I could kill him, for meanwhile we had dropped to an altitude of about 900 feet. However, the Englishman defended himself exactly as did his countryman in the morning. He fought until he landed. When he had come to the ground I flew over him at an altitude of about thirty-feet in order to ascertain whether I had killed him or not. What did the rascal do? He took his machine-gun and shot holes into my machine.

---

*It is well to note how often von Richthofen refers to the wind being in his favour. A west wind means that while the machines are fighting they are driven steadily over the German lines. Then, if the British machine happens to be inferior in speed or manœuverability to the German, and is forced down low, the pilot has the choice only of fighting to a finish and being killed, or of landing and being made prisoner. The prevalence of west winds has, for this reason, cost the R.F.C. a very great number of casualties in killed and missing, who, if the fight had occurred over territory held by the British, would merely have landed till the attacking machine had taken itself off. For similar reasons, the fact that the R.F.C. has always been on the offensive, and so has always been flying over the German lines has caused many casualties. Under all the circumstances it is surprising that the R.F.C. casualties have not been a great deal heavier.

117

Afterwards Voss told me if that had happened to him he would have shot the aviator on the ground. As a matter of fact I ought to have done so, for he had not surrendered. He was one of the few fortunate fellows who escaped with their lives.

I felt very merry, flew home and celebrated my thirty-third aeroplane.

MY RECORD DAY

The weather was glorious. We were ready for starting. I had for visitor a gentleman who had never seen a fight in the air or anything resembling it, and he had just assured me that it would tremendously interest him to witness an aerial battle.

We climbed into our packing cases, and laughed much about him. Friend Schäfer* thought that we might give him some fun. We placed him before a telescope and off we went.

The day began well. We had scarcely gone to an altitude of 6,000 feet when an English patrol of five machines was coming our way. We attacked them by a rush as if we were cavalry, and the hostile squadron lay destroyed on the ground. None of our men was even wounded. Of our enemies three had plunged to the ground, and two had come down in flames.

The good fellow down below was not a little surprised. He had imagined that the affair would look quite different, that it would be far more dramatic. He thought the whole encounter had looked quite harmless until suddenly some machines came falling down looking like rockets. I have

*Schäfer was also shot by Lieut. Rhys-Davids, R.F.C., later in 1917.

gradually become accustomed to seeing machines falling down, but I must say it impressed me very deeply when I saw my first Englishman fall, and I have often seen the event again in my dreams.

As the day had begun so propitiously we sat down and had a decent breakfast. Of course all of us were as hungry as wolves. In the meantime our machines were again made ready for starting. Fresh cartridges were got, and then we went off again.

In the evening we were able to send off the proud report: "Six German machines have destroyed thirteen hostile aeroplanes."*

Boelcke's Squadron had only once been able to make a similar report. At that time we had shot down eight machines. To-day one of us had brought low four of his opponents. The hero was a Lieutenant Wolff, a delicate-looking little fellow, in whom nobody could have suspected a redoubtable hero. My brother had destroyed two, Schäfer two, Festner two, and I three.

We went to bed in the evening tremendously proud, but also terribly tired. On the following day we read with noisy approval about our deeds of the previous day in the Official Communiqué. On the next day we downed eight hostile machines.

A very amusing thing occurred. One of the Englishmen whom we had shot down and whom we had made a prisoner was talking to us. Of course he inquired after the Red Aeroplane. It is not unknown even among the troops in the trenches, and is called by them "le diable rouge." In the squadron to which he belonged there was a rumour that the

---

*It is possible that the figures are correct. Early in 1917, before the advent of the Bristol Fighters and de Havillands in quantities, the R.F.C. was having a very bad time. On April 7, for example, it was reported in the British G.H.Q. Communiqué that 28 of our machines were missing.

Red Machine was occupied by a girl, by a kind of Jeanne d'Arc. He was intensely surprised when I assured him that the supposed girl was standing in front of him. He did not intended to make a joke. He was actually convinced that only a girl could sit in the extravagantly painted machine.

"MORITZ"

The most beautiful being in all creation is the genuine Danish hound my "little lap-dog," my "Moritz." I bought him in Ostend from a brave Belgian for five marks. His mother was a beautiful animal, and one of his fathers also was pure bred. I am convinced of that. I was allowed to select one of the litter, and I chose the prettiest. Zeumer took another puppy and called it "Max."*

Max came to a sudden end. He was run over by a motor car. Moritz flourished exceedingly. He slept with me in my bed and received a most excellent education. He never left me while I was in Ostend, and obtained my entire affection. Month by month Moritz grew, and gradually my tender little lap-dog became a colossal great beast.

Once I even took him up with me. He was my first observer. He behaved very sensibly. He seemed much interested in everything, and looked at the world from above. Only my mechanics were dissatisfied when they had to clean the machine. Afterwards Moritz was very merry.

Moritz is more than a year old, and he is still as child-like as

*The famous performing monkeys "Max and Moritz" will be green in the memories of all frequenters of music-halls and other places where they sing. These intelligent apes had a high reputation all over Europe, and, being of German origin, one imagines that they were interned along with their fellow-countrymen, if in England at the outbreak of war.

if he were still in his teens. He is very fond of playing billiards. In doing this he has destroyed many billiard balls, and particularly many a billiard cloth. He was a great passion for the chase. My mechanics are very pleased with his sporting inclinations, for he has caught for them many a nice hare. I do not much approve of his hunting proclivities. Consequently he gets a whacking if I catch him at it.

He has a silly peculiarity. He likes to accompany the flying machines at the start. The normal death of a flying-man's dog is death from the propeller. One fine day he rushed again in front of a flying machine which had been started. Of course the aeroplane caught him up, and a beautiful propeller was smashed to bits. Moritz howled terribly, and a measure which I had hitherto omitted was taken. I had always refused to have his ears cut. One of his ears was cut off by the propeller. A long ear and a short ear do not go well together.

Moritz has taken a very sensible view of the world-war and of our enemies. When, in summer 1916, he saw for the first time Russian natives – the train had stopped and Moritz was being taken for a walk – he chased the Russian crowd with loud barking. He has no great opinion of Frenchmen, although he is after all a Belgian. Once when I settled in my new quarters I ordered the people to clean the house. When I came back in the evening nothing had been done. I got angry, and asked the Frenchman to come and see me. When he opened the door Moritz greeted him rather brusquely. Immediately I understood why no cleaning had been done.

THE ENGLISH ATTACK OUR AERODROME

Nights in which the full moon is shining are most suitable for night flying.

During the full moon nights of the month of April, 1917, our English friends were particularly industrious. Of course, that had to do with the Battle of Arras. Probably they had found out that we had comfortably installed ourselves on a beautiful large flying ground at Douai.

One fine night when we were in the Officers' Mess the telephone started ringing and we were told: "The English are coming." There was of course a great hullabaloo. We had bomb-proof shelters. They had been got ready by our excellent Simon. Simon is our architect, surveyor and builder.

We dived down into shelter and we heard actually, at first very gentle humming and then the noise of an engine. The searchlights had apparently got notice at the same time, for they started getting ready.

The enemy was still too far away to be attacked. We were particularly merry. The only thing we feared was that the English would not succeed in finding our aerodrome. To find some fixed spot at night is by no means easy. It was particularly difficult to find us because our aerodrome was not situated on an important highway or near water or railway, by which one can be guided during one's flight at night.*

The Englishman was apparently flying at a great altitude. At first he circled around our entire establishment. We began to think that he had given up and was looking for another objective. Suddenly we noticed that he had switched off the engine. So he was coming lower. Wolff said: "Now the matter is becoming serious."

We had two carbines and began shooting at the

---

*This might be a useful hint to some people who like to build repair depots, or big bombing aerodromes, right alongside the sea a few miles behind the firing line, so that they may be easily located after the shortest possible flight by the most inexperienced bombing pilot.

Englishman. We could not see him. Still the noise of our shooting was a sedative to our nerves.

Suddenly he was taken up by the search-lights. There was shouting all over the flying ground. Our friend was sitting in a prehistoric packing case.* We could clearly recognise the type. He was half a mile away from us and was flying straight towards us.

He went lower and lower. At last he had come down to an altitude of about 300 feet. Then he started his engine again and came straight towards the spot where we were standing.

Wolff thought that he took an interest in the other side of our establishment, and before long the first bomb fell and it was followed by a number of others.

Our friend amused us with very pretty fireworks. They could have frightened only a coward. Broadly speaking, I find that bomb-throwing at night has only a moral effect. Those who have funk are strongly affected when bombs are falling at night. The others don't care.

We were very amused at the Englishman's performance and thought the English would come quite often on a visit. The flying piano dropped its bombs at last from an altitude of 150 feet. That was rather impertinent, for on a moonlit night I think I can hit with a rifle at 150 feet a wild pig at the chosen spot. Why then should I not succeed in hitting the Englishman? It would have been a novelty to down an English airman from the ground.

From above I had already had the honour of downing a number of Englishmen, but I had never tried to tackle an aviator from below.

When the Englishman had gone we went back to mess and discussed among ourselves how we should receive the

*One assumes that the reference is to the F.E. 2b. "pusher" biplane, which, though produced in 1915, was still used for night bombing up till well on in 1918.

English should they pay us another visit on the following night. In the course of the next day our orderlies and other fellows had to work with great energy. They had to ram into the ground piles which were to be used as a foundation for machine-guns during the coming night.

We went to the butts and tried the English machine guns which we had taken from the enemy, arranged the sights for night shooting and were very curious as to what was going to happen. I will not betray the number of our machine-guns. Anyhow, they were to be sufficient for the purpose. Every one of my officers was armed with such an implement.

We were again sitting at mess. Of course we were discussing the problem of the night fliers. Suddenly an orderly rushed in shouting: "They are there! They are there!" And disappeared into the next bomb-proof in his scanty attire. We all rushed to our machine-guns. Some of the men who were known to be good shots had also been given a machine-gun. All the rest were provided with carbines. The whole squadron was armed to the teeth to give a warm reception to our kindly visitors.

The first Englishman arrived, exactly as on the previous evening, at a very great altitude. He went then down to 150 feet and, to our greatest joy, was making for the place where our barracks were. He got into the glare of the search-light.

When he was only 300 yards away someone fired the first shot and all the rest of us joined in. A rush of cavalry or of storming troops could not have been met more efficiently than the attack of that single impertinent individual flying at 150 feet.

Quick firing from many guns received him. Of course he could not hear the noise of the machine-guns. The roar of his motor prevented that. However, he must have seen the flashes of our guns. Therefore I considered it tremendously plucky that our man did not swerve but continued going straight ahead in accordance with his plan. He flew exactly over our heads.*

At the moment when he was perpendicularly above us we jumped of course quickly into our bomb-proof. It would have been too silly for flying men to die by a rotten bomb.

As soon as he had passed over our heads we rushed out again and fired after him with our machine-guns and rifles.

Friend Schäfer asserted of course that he had hit the man. Schäfer is quite a good shot. Still, in this case I did not believe him. Besides, every one of us had as good a chance at making a hit as he had.

We had achieved something, for the enemy had dropped his bombs rather aimlessly owing to our shooting. One of them, it is true, had exploded only a few yards from the "petit rouge," but had not hurt him.

During the night the fun recommenced several times. I was already in bed, fast asleep, when I heard in a dream anti-aircraft firing. I woke up and discovered that the dream was reality. One of the Englishmen flew at so low an altitude over my habitation that in my fright I pulled the blanket over my head. The next moment I heard an incredible bang just outside my window. The panes had fallen a victim to the bomb. I rushed out of my room in my shirt in order to fire a few shots after him. They were firing from everywhere. Unfortunately, I had overslept my opportunity.

The next morning we were extremely surprised and delighted to discover that we had shot down from the ground no fewer than three Englishmen. They had landed not far from our aerodrome and had been made prisoners.

As a rule we had hit the engines and had forced the airmen to come down on our side of the Front. After all, Schäfer was

*This description is typical of what these extraordinary night-flying pilots do with their ancient "flying pianos" night after night, when the weather is reasonable. Von Richthofen's generous admiration is thoroughly well deserved.

possibly right in his assertion. At any rate, we were very satisfied with our success. The English were distinctly less satisfied, for they preferred avoiding our aerodrome. It was a pity that they gave us a wide berth, for they gave us lots of fun. Let us hope that they come back to us next month.

SCHÄFER LANDS BETWEEN THE LINES

We went on a shooting expedition on the 20th of April. We came home very late and lost Schäfer on the way.

Of course everyone hoped that he would come to hand before dark. It struck nine, it struck ten, but no Schäfer was visible. His petrol could not last so long. Consequently, he had landed somewhere, for no one was willing to admit that he had been shot down. No one dared to mention the possibility. Still, everyone was afraid for him.

The ubiquitous telephone was set in motion in order to find out whether a flying man had come down anywhere. Nobody could give us information. No Division and no Brigade had seen anything of him. We felt very uncomfortable. At last we went to bed. All of us were perfectly convinced that he would turn up in the end.

At two o'clock, after midnight, I was suddenly awakened. The telephone orderly, beaming with pleasure, reported to me: "Lieutenant Schäfer is in the village of Y—, and would like to be fetched home."

The next morning when we were sitting at breakfast the door opened and my dear pilot stood before me. His clothes were as filthy as those of an infantryman who has fought at Arras for a fortnight. He was greeted with a general Hurrah! Schäfer was tremendously happy and elated, and he had to tell us of his adventure. When he had finished

126

his breakfast he told us the following tale:

"I was flying along the front intending to return home. Suddenly I noticed far below me something that looked like an infantry flier. I attacked him, shot him down, and meant to fly back. However, the English in the trenches did not mean me to get away and started peppering me like anything. My salvation lay in the speed of my machine, for those rascals, of course, would forget that they had to aim far in front of me if they wished to hit me.

"I was at an altitude of perhaps 600 feet. Suddenly, I heard a smash and my engine stopped running. There was nothing to do but to land. I asked myself whether I should be able to get away from the English position. It seemed very questionable. The English noticed my predicament and started shooting like mad.

"As my engine was no longer running I could hear every single shot. The position became awkward. I came down and landed. Before my machine had come to a standstill they squirted upon me heaps of bullets from machine-guns in the hedge of the village of Monchy near Arras. My machine became splashed with bullets.

"I jumped out of the old box and down into the first shell hole. Squatting there I reflected and tried to realise where exactly I was. Gradually it became clear to me that I had landed outside the English lines, but damnably near them. Happily it was rather late in the evening, and that was my salvation.

"Before long the first shells came along. Of course they were gas shells and I had no mask with me. My eyes started watering like anything. Before darkness set in the English ascertained the distance of the spot where I had landed with machine-guns. Part of them aimed at my machine and part at my shell crater. The bullets constantly hit its rim.

"In order to quieten my nerves I lit a cigarette. Then I took off my heavy fur coat and prepared everything for a leap and a run. Every minute seemed to me an hour.

"Gradually it became dark, but only very gradually. Around me I heard partridges giving a concert. As an experienced shot I recognised from their voices that they felt quite happy and contented, that there was no danger of my being surprised in my hiding place.

"At last it became quite dark. Suddenly and quite close to me a couple of partridges flew up. A second couple followed. It was obvious that danger was approaching. No doubt a patrol was on the way to wish me a happy evening.

"I had no time to lose. Now or never. First I crept very cautiously on my chest from shell hole to shell hole. After creeping industriously for about an hour and a half I noticed I was nearing humans. Were they English or were they Germans? They came nearer and I could almost have fallen round their necks when I discovered our own musketeers. They were a German patrol who were nosing about in No Man's Land.

"One of the men conducted me to the Commander of his Company. I was told that in the evening I had landed about fifty yards in front of the enemy lines and that our infantry had given me up for lost. I had a good supper and then I started on my way home. Behind me there was far more shooting than in front of me. Every path, every trench, every bush, every hollow way, was under enemy fire. The English attacked on the next morning, and consequently, they had to begin their artillery preparation the evening before. So I had chosen an unfavourable day for my enterprise. I reached the first telephone only at two o'clock in the morning, when I telephoned to the squadron."

We were all very happy to have our Schäfer again with us. He went to bed. Any other man would have taken a rest from flying for twenty-four hours. But friend Schäfer attacked on the afternoon of this very day a low-flying B.E. above Monchy.

VI

THE ANTI-RICHTHOFEN CIRCUS

THE English had hit upon a splendid joke. The intended to catch me or to bring me down. For that purpose they had actually organised a special squadron which flew about in that part which we frequented as a rule. We discovered its particular aim by the fact that its aggressive activity was principally directed against our red machines.

I would say that all the machines of the whole Squadron had been painted red because our English friends had by-and-by perceived that I was sitting in a blood-red band-box. Suddenly there was quite a lot of red machines, and the English opened their eyes wide when one fine day they saw a dozen red barges steaming along instead of a single one. Our new trick did not prevent them from making an attempt at attacking us. I preferred their new tactics. It is better that one's customers come to one's shop than to have to look for one's customers abroad.

We flew to the lines hoping to find our enemy. After about twenty minutes the first arrived and attacked us. That had not happened to us for a long time. The English had abandoned their celebrated offensive tactics to some extent. They had found them somewhat too expensive.

Our aggressors were three Spads, one-seater machines. Their occupants thought themselves very superior to us because of the excellence of their apparatus. Wolff, my brother and I, were flying together. We were three against three. That was as it ought to be.

Immediately at the beginning of the encounter the aggressive became a defensive. Our superiority became clear. I tackled my opponent and could see how my brother and Wolff handled each their own enemy. The usual waltzing began. We were circling around one another. A favourable wind came to our aid. It drove us fighting away from the Front in the direction of Germany.

My man was the first who fell. I suppose I had smashed up his engine. At any rate, he made up his mind to land. I no longer give pardon to anyone. Therefore, I attacked him a second time and the consequence was that his whole machine went to pieces. His planes dropped off like pieces of paper and the body of the machine fell like a stone, burning fiercely. It dropped into a morass. It was impossible to dig it out, and I have never discovered the name of my opponent. He had disappeared. Only the end of the tail was visible and marked the place where he had dug his own grave.

Simultaneously with me, Wolff and my brother had attacked their opponents and had forced them to land not far from my victim.

We were very happy and flew home and hoped that the anti-Richthofen Squadron would often return to the fray.*

---

*One can find no trace of any deliberate attempt to organise an anti-Richthofen Circus in the R.F.C., and therefore one assumes that these were merely three gallant lads on new type Spads who went out deliberately on their own account to look for trouble, and found more than they expected.

A VISIT FROM OUR FATHER

Our father had announced that he would visit his two sons on the 29th of April. He is commander of a little town in the vicinity of Lille. Therefore he does not live very far away from us. I have occasionally seen him on my flights.

He intended to arrive by train at nine o'clock. At half-past nine he came to our aerodrome. We just happened to return from an expedition. My brother was the first to climb out of his machine, and he greeted the old gentleman with the words: "Good day, father. I have just shot down an Englishman." Immediately after, I also climbed out of my machine and greeted him: "Good day, father. I have just shot down an Englishman." The old gentleman felt very happy and he was delighted. That was obvious. He is not one of those fathers who are afraid for their sons. I think he would like best to get himself into a machine and help us shooting. We breakfasted with him and then we went again flying.

In the meantime, an aerial fight took place above our aerodrome. My father looked on and was greatly interested. We did not take a hand in the fight, for we were standing on the ground and looked on ourselves.

An English squadron had broken through and was being attacked above our aerodrome by some of our own recon-noitring aeroplanes. Suddenly one of the machines started turning over and over. Then it recovered itself and came gliding down normally. We saw with regret that this time it was a German machine.

The Englishman flew on. The German aeroplane had apparently been damaged. It was quite correctly handled. It came down and tried to land on our flying ground. The room was rather narrow for the large machine. Besides, the ground was unfamiliar to the pilot. Hence, the landing was

131

not quite smooth. We ran towards the aeroplane and discovered with regret that one of the occupants of the machine, the machine-gunner, had been killed. The spectacle was new to my father. It made him serious.

The day promised to be a favourable one for us. The weather was wonderfully clear. The anti-aircraft guns were constantly audible. Obviously, there were many aircraft about.

Towards mid-day we flew once more. This time, I was again lucky and shot down my second Englishman of the day. My father recovered his good spirits.

After the mid-day dinner I slept a little. I was again quite fresh. Wolff had fought the enemy in the meantime with his group of machines and had himself bagged an enemy. Schäfer also had beaten one. In the afternoon my brother and I, accompanied by Schäfer, Festner and Allmenröder, flew twice more.

The first afternoon flight was a failure. The second was all the better. Soon after we had come to the lines a hostile squadron met us. Unfortunately they were at a higher altitude, so we could not do anything. We tried to climb to their level, but did not succeed. We had to let them go.*

We flew along the lines. My brother was next to me, in front of the others. Suddenly I noticed two hostile artillery fliers approaching our front in the most impertinent and provocative manner. I waved to my brother and he understood my meaning. We flew side by side increasing our speed. Each of us felt certain that he was superior to the enemy. It was a great thing that we could absolutely rely on one another, and that was the principal thing. One has to know one's flying partner.

My brother was the first to approach his enemy. He

*This appears to be the first admission that the newer British machines could out-climb the famous Albatros chasers.

attacked the first and I took care of the second. At the last moment I quickly looked round in order to feel sure that there was no third aeroplane about. We were alone and could see eye to eye. Soon I had got on the favourable side of my opponent. A short spell of quick firing and the enemy machine went to pieces. I never had a more rapid success.

While I was still looking where my enemy's fragments were falling, I noticed my brother. He was scarcely 500 yards away from me and was still fighting his opponent.

I had time to study the struggle, and must say that I myself could not have done any better than he did. He had rushed his man and both were turning around one another. Suddenly, the enemy machine reared. That is a certain indication of a hit. Probably the pilot was shot in the head. The machine fell and the planes of the enemy apparatus went to pieces. They fell quite close to my victim. I flew towards my brother and we congratulated one another by waving. We were highly satisfied with our performance and flew off. It is a splendid thing when one can fly together with one's brother and do so well.

In the meantime, the other fellows of the squadron had drawn near and were watching the spectacle of the fight of the two brothers. Of course they could not help us, for only one man can shoot down an opponent. If one airman has tackled his enemy the others cannot assist. They can only look on and protect his back. Otherwise, he might be attacked in the rear.

We flew on and went to a higher altitude, for there was apparently a meeting somewhere in the air for the members of the Anti-Richthofen Club. They could recognise us from far away. In the powerful sunlight, the beautiful red colour of our machines could be seen at a long distance.

We closed our ranks, for we knew that our English friends pursued the same business as we. Unfortunately, they were again too high. So we had to wait for their attack. The celebrated Sopwith triplanes and Spads were new machines. However, the quality of the box matters little. Success depends upon the man who sits in it. The English airmen played a cautious game but would not bite. We offered to fight them, either on one side of the lines or on the other. But they said, "No, thank you." What is the good of bringing out a squadron against us and then turning tail?*

At last, one of the men plucked up courage and dropped down upon our rear machine. Naturally battle was accepted, although our position was unfavourable. If one wishes to do business one must, after all, adapt oneself to the desires of one's customers. Therefore we all turned round. The Englishman noticed what was going on and got away. A commencement had been made.

Another Englishman tried a similar trick on me and I greeted him at once with quick fire from my two machine-guns. He tried to escape me by dropping down. That was fatal to him. When he got beneath me I remained on top of him. Everything in the air that is beneath me, especially if it is a one-seater, a chaser, is lost, for it cannot shoot to the rear.

My opponent had a very good and very fast machine. However, he did not succeed in reaching the English lines. I began to fire at him when we were above Lens. I started shooting when I was much too far away. That was merely a trick of mine. I did not mean so much to hit him as to frighten him, and I succeeded in catching him. He began flying curves and this enabled me to draw near. I tried the same manoeuvre a second and a third time. Every time my foolish friend started making his curves. So I had gradually edged quite close to him.

*The probability is that the British machines being high up, and watching the sky all round, did not notice the little red machines against the dark ground below them for some time.

134

I approached him almost to touching distance. I aimed very carefully. I waited a moment, and when I was at most at a distance of 50 yards from him I started with both the machine-guns at the same time. I heard a slight hissing noise, a certain sign that the petrol tanks had been hit. Then I saw a bright flame and my lord disappeared below.

This was the fourth victim of the day. My brother bagged two. Apparently, we had invited our father to a treat. His joy was wonderful.

I had invited several gentlemen for the evening. Among these was my dear Wedel, who happened to be in the neighbourhood. We had a great treat. The two brothers had bagged six Englishmen in a single day. That is a whole Flying Squadron.*

I believe the English cease to feel any liking for us.†

I FLY HOME

I had shot down fifty aeroplanes. That was a nice number, but I would have preferred fifty-two. So I went up one day and had another two, although it was against orders.

As a matter of fact I had been allowed to bag only forty-one. Anyone will be able to guess why the number was fixed at forty-one. Just for that reason I wanted to avoid that figure. I am not out for breaking records. Besides, generally speaking, we of the Flying Service do not think of records at all. We merely think of our duty. Boelcke might have shot down a hundred aeroplanes but for his accident, and many

---

*A whole squadron is 18 machines, divided into 3 "flights" of 6 machines each. The word squadron does not, apparently, translate exactly into German.

†Nevertheless, some months after this, a young British pilot was being entertained one evening by his squadron in celebration of his having been awarded the D.S.O., and when called upon for a speech proposed the health of von Richthofen. And the squadron duly honoured the toast.

others of our dear dead comrades might have vastly increased their bag but for their sudden death. Still, it is some fun to have downed half a hundred aeroplanes. After all, I had succeeded in obtaining permission to bring down fifty machines before going on leave.

I hope that I may live to celebrate a second lot of fifty.

In the evening of that particular day the telephone bell was ringing. Headquarters wished to speak to me. It seemed to me the height of fun to be connected with the holy of holies.

They gave me over the wire the cheerful news that His Majesty had expressed the wish to make my personal acquaintance, and had fixed the date for me. I had to make an appearance on the 2nd of May. The notification reached me on the 30th of April at nine o'clock in the evening. I should not have been able to fulfil the wish of our All-Highest War-Lord by taking the train. I therefore thought I would travel by air, especially as that mode of locomotion is far pleasanter. I started the next morning, not in my single-seater ''le petit rouge'' but in a big fat two-seater.

I took a seat at the rear, not at the stick. The man who had to do the flying was Lieut. Krefft, one of the officers of my squadron. He was just going on leave to recover his strength. So things fitted in admirably. He also got home quicker travelling by air and he preferred the trip by aeroplane.

I started on the journey rather hastily. The only luggage which I took with me was my tooth-brush. Therefore, I had to dress for the journey in the clothes in which I was to appear at Headquarters. Now, a soldier does not carry with him many beautiful uniforms when he goes to war, and the scarcity of nice clothes is particularly great in the case of a poor ''Front-hog'' like myself.

My brother undertook the command of the aeroplane

squadron in my absence. I took leave with a few words, for I hoped soon to recommence my work among those dear fellows.

The route was via Namur, Liège, Aix la Chapelle and Cologne. It was lovely for once to sail through the air without any thoughts of war. The weather was wonderful. We had rarely had such a perfect time. Probably the men at the Front would be extremely busy.

Soon our own captive balloons were lost to sight The thunder of the Battle of Arras was only heard in the distance. Beneath us all was peace. We saw steamers on the rivers and fast trains on the railways. We overtook easily everything below. The wind was in our favour. The earth seemed as flat as a threshing floor. The beautiful mountains of the Meuse were not recognisable as mountains. One could not even trace them by their shadows, for the sun was right above us. We only knew that they were there, and with a little imagination we could hide ourselves in the cool glades of that delightful country.

It had become late. Clouds were gathering below and hid from us the earth. We flew on, taking our directions by means of the sun and the compass. The vicinity of Holland was disagreeable to us. So we thought we should go lower in order to find out where we were. We went beneath the cloud and discovered that we were above Namur.

We then went on to Aix la Chapelle. We left that town to our left and about mid-day we reached Cologne. We both were in high spirits. We had before us a long leave of absence. The weather was beautiful. We had succeeded in all our undertakings. We had reached Cologne. We could be certain to get in time to Headquarters, whatever might happen.

Our coming had been announced in Cologne by telegram. People were looking out for us. On the previous day

137

the newspapers had reported my fifty-second aerial victory. One can imagine what kind of a reception they had prepared for us.

Having been flying for three hours I had a slight headache. Therefore, I thought I would take forty winks, before going to Headquarters. From Cologne we flew along the Rhine for some distance. I knew the country well. I had often journeyed that way by steamer, by motor car, and by railway, and now I was travelling by aeroplane. It is difficult to say which of these is the most pleasant form of locomotion. Of course, one can see better the details of the landscape from the steamer. However, the commanding review one gets from an aeroplane has also its attractions. The Rhine is a very beautiful river also from above.

We flew rather low in order not to lose the sensation that we were travelling among mountains. For after all the most beautiful part of the Rhine are the tree-clad hills, castles, etc. Of course we could not make out individual houses. It is a pity that one cannot fly slowly as well as quickly. If it had been possible I would have flown quite slowly.

The beautiful views which we saw vanished only too quickly. Nevertheless, when one flies high in the air one never has the sensation that one is proceeding at a fast pace. If one is sitting in a motor car or in a fast train one has the impression of tremendous speed. On the other hand, one seems to be advancing slowly when one flies in an aeroplane at a considerable speed. One notices the celerity of one's progress only when one has not looked out of the machine for four or five minutes and then tries to find out where one has got to. Then the aspect of the country appears suddenly completely changed. The territory which one passed over a little while ago looks quite different from a different angle. One does not recognise the scenery one has passed. Herein lies the reason that an aviator can easily lose his way if he forgets for a moment to examine the territory.

In the afternoon we arrived at Headquarters and were cordially received by some comrades with whom I was acquainted and who worked at the Holiest of Holies. I absolutely pity those poor ink-spillers. They get only half the fun in war.

First of all I went to the General Commanding the Flying Services.

On the next morning came the great moment when I was to meet von Hindenburg and von Ludendorf. I had to wait for quite a while.

I should find it difficult to describe my encounter with these Generals. I saw von Hindenburg first and then von Ludendorf.

It is a weird feeling to be in the room where the fate of the world is decided. So I was quite glad when I was again outside the Holiest of Holies and when I had been commanded to lunch with His Majesty. The day was the day of my birth, and somebody had apparently told His Majesty. He congratulated me in the first place on my success, and in the second, on my twenty-fifth birthday. At the same time he handed me a birthday present.

Formerly I would never have believed it possible that on my twenty-fifth birthday I would be sitting at the right of General Field Marshal von Hindenburg and that I would be mentioned by him in a speech.

On the day following I was to take mid-day dinner with the Kaiserin. And so I went to Homburg. Her Majesty also gave me a birthday present, and I had the great pleasure to show her how to start an aeroplane. In the evening I was again invited by General Field Marshal von Hindenburg. The day following I flew to Freiburg to do some shooting. At Freiburg I made use of a machine which was going to

Berlin by air. In Nuremberg I replenished my tanks with petrol. A thunderstorm was coming on. I was in a great hurry to get to Berlin. Various more or less interesting things awaited me there. So I flew on, the thunderstorm notwithstanding. I enjoyed the clouds and the beastly weather. The rain fell in streams. Sometimes it hailed. Afterwards the propeller had the most extraordinary aspect. The hailstones had damaged it considerably. The blades looked like saws.

Unfortunately I enjoyed the bad weather so much that I quite forgot looking about me. When I remembered that one has to look out it was too late. I had no longer any idea where I was. That was a nice position to be in! I had lost my way in my own country! My people at home would laugh when they knew it! However, there it was and could not be helped. I had no idea where I was. Owing to a powerful wind I had been driven out of my course and off my map. Guided by sun and compass, I tried to get the direction of Berlin.

Towns, villages, hills and forests were slipping away below me. I did not recognise a thing. I tried in vain to compare the picture beneath with my map. Everything was different. I found it impossible to recognise the country. Later on I discovered the impossibility of finding my way, for I was flying about sixty miles outside my map.

After having flown for a couple of hours my guide and I resolved to land somewhere in the open. That is always unpleasant. One cannot tell how the surface of the ground is in reality. If one of the wheels get into a hole one's box is converted into matchwood.

We tried to read the name written up on a station, but of course that was impossible. It was too small. So we had to land. We did it with a heavy heart, for nothing else could be done. We looked for a meadow which appeared suitable from above and tried our luck. Closer inspection unfortunately showed that the meadow was not as pleasant as it seemed. That fact was obviously proved by the bent frame of our machine. We had made ourselves gloriously ridiculous. We had first lost our way and then smashed the apple cart. So we had to continue our journey with a commonplace conveyance, by railway train. Slow but sure, we reached Berlin. We had landed in the neighbourhood of Leipzig. If we had not landed so stupidly, we would certainly have reached Berlin. But sometimes one makes a mistake whatever one does.

Some days later I arrived in Schweidnitz, my own town. Although I got there at seven o'clock in the morning, there was a large crowd at the station. I was very cordially received. In the afternoon various demonstrations took place to honour me, among others, one of the local Boy Scouts.

It became clear to me that the people at home took after all a vivid interest in their fighting soldiers.

MY BROTHER

I had not yet passed eight days of my leave when I received the telegram: "Lothar is wounded, but not mortally." That was all. Inquiries showed that he had been very rash. He flew against the enemy together with Allmenröder. Beneath him and a good distance on the other side of the lines, he saw in the air a lonely Englishman crawling about. He was one of those hostile infantry fliers who make themselves particularly disagreeable to our troops. We molest them a great deal. Whether they really achieve anything in crawling along the ground is very problematical.*

My brother was at an altitude of about 6,000 feet, while the Englishman was at about 3,000 feet. He quietly approached the Englishman, prepared to plunge, and in a few seconds was upon him. Englishman thought he would avoid a duel, and he disappeared likewise by a plunge. My brother, without hesitation, plunged after. He didn't care at all whether he was on one side of the lines or the other. He was animated by a single thought: "I must down that fellow!" That is, of course, the correct way of managing things. Now and then I myself acted that way. However, if my brother does not have at least one success on every flight he gets tired of the whole thing.

Only a little above the ground my brother obtained a favourable position towards the English flier, and could shoot into his shop windows. The Englishman falls. There is nothing more to be done.

After such a struggle, especially at a low altitude, in the course of which one has so often been twisting and turning, and circling to the right and to the left, the average mortal has no longer the slightest notion of his position. On that day it happened that the air was somewhat misty. The weather was particularly unfavourable. My brother took quickly his bearings, and discovered only now that he was a long distance behind the Front. He was behind the ridge of Vimy. The top of that hill is about 300 feet higher than the country around. My brother, so the observers on the ground reported, had disappeared behind the Vimy height.

*Probably the fighting to the east of Amiens in March and April 1918 has demonstrated to the German Army at large that quite a great deal is achieved by this "crawling along the ground." The use of aeroplanes against infantry and cavalry has been developed very greatly since von Richthofen wrote his notes in 1917.

It is not a particularly pleasant feeling to fly home over enemy country. One is shot at and cannot shoot back. It is true a hit is rare. My brother approached the line. At a low altitude one can hear every shot that is fired, and firing sounds then very much like the noise made by chestnuts which are being roasted. Suddenly, he felt that he had been hit. That was queer to him.

My brother is one of those men who cannot bear to see their own blood. Somebody else bleeding would not impress him very greatly, but the sight of his own blood upsets him.* He felt how his blood was running down his right leg in a warm stream. At the same time he noticed pain in his hip. Below the shooting continued. It followed that he was still over hostile ground.

At last the firing gradually ceased. He had crossed the lines. Now he had to be quick, for his strength was rapidly ebbing away. He saw a wood and next to the wood a meadow. Therefore, he made straight for the meadow. Acting mechanically he switched off the engine. At the same moment he lost consciousness.

My brother was in a single-seater. No one could help him. It is a miracle how he came to the ground. For no flying machine lands or starts automatically. There is a rumour that they have at Cologne an old school Taube which from sheer force of habit will start by itself as soon as the pilot takes his seat, which makes the regulation curve and which lands again after exactly five minutes.** Many men pretend having seen that miraculous machine. I have not seen it. But still I am convinced that the tale is true.

*This is a rather interesting psychological fact. The dislike of seeing one's own blood does not entail cowardice, but it is recognised that some men do become considerably upset at the sight.

 **Curiously enough there is a very similar legend concerning an aged school machine at one of the British flying schools.

Now, my brother was not in such a miraculous automatic machine. Nevertheless he had not hurt himself in landing. He recovered consciousness only in hospital, and was sent to Douai.

It is a curious feeling to see one's brother fighting with an Englishman. For instance, once I saw that Lothar, who was hanging behind the squadron, was being attacked by an English aviator. It would have been easy for him to avoid battle. He need only plunge. But he would not do that. That would not even occur to him. He does not know how to run away. Happily I had observed what was going on, and was looking for my chance.

I noticed how the Englishman went for my brother and shot at him. My brother tried to reach the Englishman's altitude disregarding the shots. Suddenly his machine turned a somersault and plunged perpendicularly, turning round and round. It was not an intended plunge, but a regular fall. That is not a nice thing to look at, especially if the falling pilot is one's own brother. Gradually I had to accustom myself to that sight, for it was one of my brother's tricks. As soon as he felt sure that the Englishman was his superior he acted as if he had been shot.

The Englishman rushed after him. My brother recovered his balance, and in a moment had got above his enemy. The hostile aeroplane could not equally quickly get ready for what was to come. My brother caught it at a favourable angle, and a few seconds after it went down in flames. When a machine is burning all is lost, for it falls to the ground burning.

Once I was on the ground next to a petrol tank. It contained 100 litres of petrol, which exploded and burnt. The heat was so great that I could not bear to be within ten yards of it. One can therefore imagine what it means if a tank containing a large quantity of this devilish liquid explodes a few inches in front of one while the blast from the propeller blows the flame into one's face. I believe one loses consciousness at the first moment.

Sometimes miracles do happen. For instance, I once saw an English aeroplane falling down in flames. The flames burst out only at an altitude of 1,500 feet. The whole machine was burning. When we had flown home we were told that one of the occupants of the machine had jumped from an altitude of 150 feet. It was the observer. 150 feet is the height of a good-sized steeple. Supposing somebody should jump from its top to the ground, what would be his condition? Most men would break their bones in jumping from a first floor window. At any rate, this good fellow jumped from a burning machine at an altitude of 150 feet, from a machine which had been burning for over a minute, and nothing happened to him except a simple fracture of the leg. Soon after his adventure he made a statement from which it appears that his nerve had not suffered.*

Another time I shot down an English machine. The pilot had been fatally wounded in the head. The machine fell perpendicularly to earth from an altitude of 9,000 feet. Some time later I came gliding down, and saw on the ground nothing but a heap of twisted débris. To my surprise I was told that the observer had only damaged his skull, and that his condition was not dangerous. Some people have luck indeed.

Once upon a time, Boelcke shot down a Nieuport machine. I was present. The aeroplane fell like a stone. When we inspected it we found that it had been driven up

*On two or three occasions pilots have gallantly stuck to their controls and have managed to land safely in blazing machines from fully 1,000 feet. There is a general opinion that it is possible to fit a parachute so that in the event of an aeroplane catching fire the pilot, and passenger – if any, – can quit it at once and descend safely.

to the middle into the loamy soil. The occupant had been shot in the abdomen, and had lost consciousness and had wrenched his arm out of its socket on striking the ground. He did not die of his fall.

On the other hand, it has happened that a good friend of mine in landing had a slight accident. One of the wheels of his machine got into a rabbit hole. The aeroplane was travelling at no speed, and quite slowly went on its head. It seemed to reflect whether it should fall to the one side or to the other, turned over and the poor fellow's back was broken.

My brother Lothar is a Lieutenant in the 4th Dragoons. Before the war he was at the War Academy. He was made an officer at the outbreak of war, and began as a cavalry-man exactly as I did. I know nothing about his actions, for he never speaks of himself. However, I have been told the following story:

In winter, 1914, Lothar's regiment was on the Warthe. The Russians were on the other side of the river. Nobody knew whether they intended to stay there or go back. The water was frozen along the shore. So it was difficult to ride through the river. There were, of course, no bridges, for the Russians had destroyed them. So my brother swam across, ascertained the position of the Russians and swam back again. He did that during a severe Russian winter when the thermometer was very low. After a few minutes his clothes were frozen solid. Yet he asserted that he felt quite warm. He kept on his horse all day long until he got to his quarters in the evening, yet he did not catch a chill.

In winter, 1915, he followed my urgent advice, and went into the Flying Service. He also became an observer, and became a pilot only a year later. Acting as an observer is certainly not a bad training, particularly for a chasing pilot. In March, 1917, he passed his third examination, and came at once to my squadron.

When he arrived he was a very young and innocent pilot who had never thought of looping and such like tricks. He was quite satisfied if he succeeded in starting his machine and in landing successfully. A fortnight later I took him with me against the enemy for the first time. I asked him to fly close behind me in order that he might see exactly how the fighting business was done.

After the third flight with him I suddenly noticed how he parted company with me. He rushed at an Englishman, and killed him. My heart leapt with joy when I saw it. The event proved once more that there is no art in shooting down an aeroplane. The thing is done by the personality or by the fighting determination of the airman.* I am not a Pégoud, and I do not wish be a Pégoud. I am only a soldier who does his duty.

Four weeks later my brother had shot down twenty Englishmen. His record as a flier is probably unique. It has probably not happened in any other case that a pilot, a fortnight after his third examination, has shot down his first enemy, and that he has shot down twenty during the first four weeks of his fighting life.

My brother's twenty-second opponent was the celebrated Captain Ball. He was by far the best English flier. Major Hawker, who in his time was as renowned as Captain Ball, I had sent home some months previously. It was a particular pleasure to me that it fell to my brother to settle England's second flying champion.

Captain Ball flew a triplane and encountered my brother flying by himself at the Front. Each tried to catch the other. Neither gave his opponent a chance. Every encounter was a short one. They were constantly dashing at one another.

*This may be the propagandist editor at work, or it may be a deliberate attempt to mislead, because, as a matter of fact, a man cannot survive long as a fighting pilot unless he is a perfect master of his machine.

147

Neither succeeded in getting behind the other. Suddenly both resolved to fire a few well-aimed shots during the few moments of the encounter. Both rushed at one another and fired. Both had before them their engine. The probability of a hit is very small, for the celerity of motion is twice as great as normally. It was improbable that either should succeed. My brother, who was a little lower, had pulled his machine around too hard, and the result was that it over-turned. For a moment his aeroplane became uncontrol-lable. But presently he recovered control, and found out that his opponent had smashed both his petrol tanks. Therefore, he had to stop the engine and land quickly. Otherwise, his machine might burst into flames.

His next idea was: What had become of my opponent? At the moment when his machine turned its somersault he had seen that the enemy's machine was rearing up in the air, and had also turned a somersault. He therefore could not be very far. His whole thought was: Is he above me or beneath me? He was not above – he saw the triplane falling down in a series of somersaults. It fell, fell, fell until it came to the ground, where it was smashed to pieces. This hap-pened on German territory. Both opponents had during the brief moment of the encounter hit one another with their machine-guns. My brother's machine had both benzine tanks smashed, and at the same moment Captain Ball had been shot through the head. He carried with him some photographs and cuttings from the newspapers of his town, where he had been greatly fêted. Apparently he had been on leave a short time before. In Boelcke's time Cap-tain Ball destroyed thirty-six German machines. He, too, had found his master. Was it by chance that a prominent man such as he should also die an ordinary soldier's death?*

*There is some curious error here, for Captain Ball was not flying a triplane at the time of his death. It seems probable that someone else shot Captain Ball on

148

Captain Ball was certainly the Commander of the Anti-Richthofen Squadron. I believe that the Englishmen will now give up their attempt to catch me. I should regret it, for in that case I should miss many nice opportunities to make myself beloved by them.

Had my brother not been wounded on the 5th of May he would probably, on my return from furlough, also have been given a leave of absence with fifty-two hostile machines to his credit.

LOTHAR, A BUTCHER, NOT A SPORTSMAN

My father discriminates between a sportsman and a butcher. The latter shoots for fun. When I have shot down an Englishman, my hunting passion is satisfied for a quarter of an hour. Therefore I do not succeed in shooting two Englishmen in succession. If one of them comes down I have the feeling of complete satisfaction. Only much, much later I have overcome my instinct, and have become a butcher.

My brother was differently constituted. I had an opportunity of observing him when he was shooting down his fourth and fifth opponents. We were attacking in a squadron. I started the dance. I had settled my opponent very quickly. When I looked around I noticed my brother rushing after an English machine which was bursting into flames, and exploded. Next to it was another Englishmen. My brother, though following No. 1, immediately directed his machine-gun against No. 2, although his first opponent

the same day, and that, as the younger von Richthofen was disabled, and so could not go and identify the wreckage of Captain Ball's machine, the credit was given to von Richthofen in default of anyone else making a claim.

149

was still in the air, and had not yet fallen. His second victim also fell after a short struggle.

When we met at home he asked me proudly: "How many have you shot down?" I said quite modestly, "One." He turned his back upon me and said. "I did two." Thereupon I sent him forward to make inquiries. He was to find out the names of his victims, etc. He returned late in the afternoon having found only a single Englishman.

He had looked carelessly, as is usual amongst such butchers. Only on the following day I received a report as to the place where the second had come down.

We all had seen his fall.

I SHOOT A BISON

When visiting Headquarters I met the Prince von Pless.* He permitted me to shoot a bison on his estate. The European bison has died out. In the whole of Europe there are only two spots where bison may be found. These are the Pless estate and in the Bialowicz estate of the ex-Czar. The Bialowicz forest has, of course, suffered terribly through the war. Many a magnificent bison, which ought to have been shot either by the Czar or by some other monarch, has been eaten by German musketeers.

Through the kindness of the Prince I was permitted to shoot so rare an animal. In a few decades none will be left.

I arrived at Pless on the afternoon of the 26th of May, and had to start immediately from the station if I wished to kill a bull the same evening. We drove along the celebrated road through the giant preserves of the Prince, which have been

*Who married Miss Cornwallis West.

150

visited by many crowned heads. After about an hour we got out, and had to walk for half an hour to come to the shooting place. The drivers had already been placed in position. The signal was given to them, and they began the drive.

I stood at an elevated spot which had been occupied, according to the head forester, by His Majesty, who from thence had shot many a bison. We waited some considerable time. Suddenly I saw among the timber a gigantic black monster, rolling along. It came straight in my direction. I noticed it before the head forester. I got ready for firing and must say that I felt somewhat nervous.

It was a mighty bull. When he was at a distance of 200 yards there was still some hope for him. I thought it was too far for a shot. Of course I could have hit the monster, because it was impossible to miss such a huge beast. However, it would have been unpleasant to search for him. Besides it would have been ridiculous had I missed him. So I thought I would wait until he came nearer.

Probably he noticed the drivers, for he suddenly turned and came rushing towards me at a sharp angle and at a speed which seemed to me incredible. It was a bad position for a shot, and in a moment he disappeared behind a group of stout trees.

I heard him snorting and stamping. I lost sight of him. I have no idea whether he smelt me or not. At any rate, he had disappeared. I caught another glimpse of him at a long distance, and he was gone.

I do not know whether it was the unaccustomed aspect of the animal or whether something else affected me. At any rate, at the moment when the bull came near I had the same feeling, the same nervousness which seizes me when I am sitting in my aeroplane and notice an Englishman at so great distance that I have to fly perhaps five minutes in order to get near him. The only difference is that the

Englishman defends himself. Possibly, different feelings would have moved me had I been standing on level ground and not on an elevated position.

Before long a second bison came near. He was also a huge fellow. He made it easier for me to fire my shot. At a distance of eighty yards I fired at him, but I had missed my opportunity to shoot him in the shoulder. A month before von Hindenburg had told me when talking of bison: "You must take a lot of cartridges with you. I have spent on such a fellow half a dozen, for he does not die easily. His heart lies so deep that one misses it as a rule." That was really so. Although I knew exactly where the bison's heart was I had missed it. I fired a second shot and a third. Hit for the third time the bull stopped perhaps fifty yards from me.

Five minutes later the beast was dead. The shooting was finished. All three bullets had hit him close above the heart.

We drove now past the beautiful hunting box of the Prince through the forest, in which the guests of Prince Pless shoot every year deer, etc. Then we looked at the interior of the house in Promnitz. It is situated on a peninsula. It commands beautiful views, and for three miles around no human being can be seen.

One has no longer the feeling that one is in a preserve of the ordinary kind when one visits the estate of Prince Pless, for the preserve extends to a million acres. It contains glorious stags which have never been seen by man. No forester knows them. Occasionally they are shot. One can tramp about for weeks without seeing a bison. During certain times of the year it is impossible to find one. They like quietude, and they can hide themselves in the gigantic forests and tangled woods. We saw many beautiful deer.

After about two hours we arrived at Pless just before dark.

INFANTRY FLIERS, ARTILLERY FLIERS, AND RECONNAISSANCE MACHINES

Had I not become a professional chaser I should have turned an Infantry flier. After all, it must be a very satisfactory feeling to be able to aid those troops whose work is hardest. The infantry flier can do a great deal to assist the man on foot. His is a very grateful task.*

In the course of the Battle of Arras I have observed many of these splendid fellows. They flew in any weather and at any time at a low altitude over the enemy, and tried to act as connecting links with our hard-pressed troops. I can understand that one can fight with enthusiasm when one is given such a task. I dare say many an airman has shouted Hurrah! as, after an assault, he saw the hostile masses stream back when our smart infantry jumped from the trenches and fought the aggressors eye to eye. Many a time, after a chasing expedition, I have fired my remaining cartridges into the enemy trenches. Although I may have done little practical good, such firing affects the enemy's morale.

I have also been an artillery flier. In my time it was a novelty to regulate the firing of one's own artillery by wireless telegraphy. To do this well an aviator requires special talent. I could not do the work for long. I prefer fighting. Very likely, artillery officers make the best artillery fliers. At least, they have the necessary knowledge of the arm which they serve.**

I have done a lot of reconnoitring by aeroplane, particularly in Russia during the war of movement. Then I acted once more like a cavalryman. The only difference was that I

*This was evidently written some time after von Richthofen's previous disparaging note on Infantry Contact patrols.
**This is an argument which a few people in this country have been trying hard to inculcate into those in authority.

rode a Pegasus made of steel. My days spent with friend Holck among the Russians were among the finest in my life. However, the war of movement seems to be ended.

In the Western theatre the eye of the reconnaissance flier sees things which are very different from those to which the cavalryman is accustomed. Villages and towns, railways and roads seem lifeless and dead. Yet there is a colossal traffic going on all the time. But it is hidden from the flying men with great skill. Only a wonderfully trained, practised and observant eye can see anything definite when one is travelling at a great height and at a terrific speed. I have excellent eyes, but it seems doubtful to me whether there is anyone who can see anything definite when he looks down upon a road from an altitude of 15,000 feet. As the eye is an imperfect object for observation one replaces it by the photographic apparatus. Everything that seems important to one must be photographed. Besides, one must photograph those things which one is told to photograph. If one comes home and if the plates have gone wrong, the whole flight has been for nothing.

It often happens to flying men who do reconnoitring that they get involved in a fight. However, their task is more important than fighting. Frequently a photographic plate is more valuable than the shooting down of a squadron. Hence the flying photographer should, as a rule, not take a hand in fighting.

Nowadays it is a difficult task to reconnoitre efficiently in the West.*

---

*This is really a high testimony to the effective work of the R.F.C.

THE GERMAN FLYING MACHINES

In the course of the war the German flying machines have experienced great changes. That is probably generally known. There is a colossal difference between a Giant Aeroplane and a Chaser Aeroplane.

The chaser plane is small, fast, quick at turning. It carries nothing apart from the pilot except machine-guns and ammunition.

The Giant Aeroplane is a colossus. Its only duty is to carry as much weight as possible, and it is able to do this owing to the huge surface of its planes. It is worth while to look at the gigantic English aeroplane* which landed smoothly on the German side of the lines.

The Giant Aeroplane can carry an unbelievable weight. It will easily fly when lifting from three to five tons. Its petrol tanks look as large as railway wagons. In going about in such a colossus one has no longer the sensation that one is flying. One is driving. In going about in a giant aeroplane the control depends no longer on one's instinct, but on the technical instruments which one carries.

A giant aeroplane has a huge amount of horse power. I do not know exactly how many, but they are in the thousands. The greater the horse power the better. It seems not impossible that the day may come when a whole division will be transported in such a thing. In its body one can go for a walk. In one of its corners there is an indescribable something. It contains an apparatus for wireless telegraphy by means of which one can converse with the people down below. In another corner are hanging the most attractive "liver sausages" which one can imagine. They are the famous bombs which cause such a fright to the good people

*A Handley Page which landed by mistake near Laon early in 1917.

down below. At every corner is a gun. The whole thing is a flying fortress, and the planes with their stays and supports look like arcades. I have never been able to find enthusiasm for these giant barges. I find them horrible, unsportsman-like, boring and clumsy. I rather like a machine of the type of "le petit rouge." If one is in a small chaser machine it is quite immaterial whether one flies on one's back, whether one flies up or down or stands on one's head. One can play any tricks one likes, for in such a machine one can fly like a bird. The only difference is that one does not fly with wings, as does the bird albatross. The thing is, after all, merely a flying engine. I think things will come to this, that we shall be able to buy a flying suit for half-a-crown. One gets into it. On the one end there is a little engine and a little airscrew. One sticks one's arms into the planes and one's legs into the tail. Then one does a few leaps in order to start, and one goes up into the air like a bird.

My dear reader, I hear you laughing at my story. But we do not know yet whether our children will laugh at it. Everyone would have laughed fifty years ago if somebody had spoken about flying above Berlin. I remember the sensation which was caused when in 1910 Zeppelin came for the first time to Berlin. Now no Berlin gutter-brat looks up into the air when an airship is coming along.

Besides Giant aeroplanes and little chaser machines, there are innumerable other types of flying machine, and they are of all sizes. Inventiveness has not yet come to an end. Who can tell what machine we shall employ a year hence in order to perforate the atmosphere?

Appendix 1
VICTORY LIST OF BARON MANFRED VON RICHTHOFEN

Norman Franks

MANY attempts to list von Richthofen's 80 victories have been made over the last seventy years. The list which follows is my latest version which even now I cannot claim to be 100% accurate. Perhaps at this distance we shall never be able to produce the definitive list.

Many of Richthofen's victories are not in dispute, for in many cases he collected the serial number from the crashed aeroplane, on other occasions the serial number is recorded in the German records. The queries are where either the machine came down in "no-man's-land" or behind the British lines, or where the machine was totally destroyed by fire and other similar aircraft fell in the vicinity of his victim.

Over the years some established victories have now been proved, or it is strongly believed, are in error. Some notation to these will appear in the list for future researchers to investigate.

I wish to acknowledge the help of the late Air Vice Marshal Raymond Collishaw CB DSO OBE DSC DFC who did much research into Richthofen's claims, and Russell Guest, another keen aviation researcher on both WW1 and WW2.

1916
1. 17 Sept	FE2b	11 Sqn 7018	Bombing Escort west of Marcoing Took off 9.10 am.
		Pilot:	2/Lt Lionel Bertram Frank Morris

				3/Royal West Surrey Rgt/RFC Died of Wounds. Aero Cert 2334, 25 Jan 1916
			Observer:	Lt T Rees, Royal Welsh Rgt/RFC Killed in Action.
2.	23 Sept	Martinsyde G100	27 Sqn 7481	Offensive Patrol (OP) Marcoing T/off 8.40 am
			Pilot:	Sgt H Bellerby Killed in Action.
3.	30 Sept	FE2b	11 Sqn 6973	Bombing Escort – Bapaume T/off 9.10 am, seen to fall in flames SE of Bapaume
			Pilot:	Lt Ernest Conway Lansdale ASC/RFC Died of Wounds as POW Age 21, son of Major E E Lansdale Arrived in France 17 Sept 1916
			Observer:	Sgt A Clarkson – Killed in Action
4.	7 Oct	BE12	21 Sqn 6618	OP Ytres, t/off 7.30 am, crashed at Equancourt.
			Pilot:	2/Lt W C Fenwick RFC(SR) Killed in Action.

5. 16 Oct BE12   19 Sqn 6580   Bomb raid, Ytres, Somme.
           Pilot: 2/Lt John Thompson RFC (GL)
                                        Aero Cert 3082, 23 May 1916

[Pilot usually referred to as Capt C R Tidswell, but he was flying BE12 No. 6620 on this day. There is also a suggestion that Lt E W Capper was killed by von Richthofen on this day, but Capper was killed in April 1917 by Kurt Wolff.]

6. 25 Oct BE12   21 Sqn 6654   OP Beaulencourt, t/off 7.45 am
           Pilot: 2/Lt W T W Wilcox, Yorks Rgt/RFC Prisoner of War; shot down near Bapaume by German biplane.

7. 3 Nov   FE2b   18 Sqn 7010   OP over Vth Army Front, t/off 11.35 am. Fell at Loupart Wood, beyond Beaumont Hamel.
           Pilot: Sgt G C Baldwin (24130)
           Observer: 2/Lt G Andrew Bentham E. Surrey Rgt & RFC, from South London. Killed in Action.

8. 9 Nov   BE2C   12 Sqn 2506   Bombing Vraucourt, t/off 8.05 am, fell at Beugny.

	Pilot:		2/Lt J G Cameron, Cameron High-l'ders & RFC. Died of Wounds. The Sqn lost 3 BEs on this raid.

9. 20 Nov BE2C   15 Sqn 2767   Artillery Observation (Art Obs)
T/off 6.50 am, seen shot down by a scout over Guedecourt.

Pilot: 2/Lt J C Lees, Royal Scts Fus/RFC Prisoner of War

Observer: Lt T H Clarke, AOD/RFC Prisoner of War.

10. 20 Nov FE2b   22 Sqn 4848   Defence Patrol, Vth Army front t/off 1.15 pm. Fell south of Grandecourt.

Pilot: 2/Lt Gilbert Sudbury Hall RFC(SR) born 1891, Aero Cert 2286, Jan 1916 To France May 1916. Died of Wounds.

Observer: 2/Lt G Doughty, Royal Scots, att'd RFC. Killed in Action.

11.	23 Nov	DH2	24 Sqn 5964	Defence Patrol 4th Army Front, t/off 1 pm.
			Pilot:	Major Lanoe George Hawker VC DSO RE & RFC; Killed in Action. Born 1890, Aero Cert No. 435, 4 March 1913.
12.	11 Dec	DH2	32 Sqn 5986	Escort, t/off 9.20 am, fell at Mercatel.
			Pilot:	Lt Philip B G Hunt, 2/1 Shrop Yeomanry & RFC. Prisoner of War. Aero Cert No. 2225 14 Dec 1915.
13.	20 Dec	DH2	29 Sqn 7927	OP to Rollencourt & Gommecourt. T/off 9.45 am, seen to fall east of Adinfer Wood.
			Pilot:	Capt Arthur Gerald Knight DSO RFC Killed in Action. Aero Cert No. 2063, 11 Nov 1915.
14.	20 Dec	FE2b	18 Sqn A5446	OP Vth Army Front, t/off 11.15 am.

			Pilot:	Lt Lionel George D'Arcy 3/Conn't Rangers & RFC. Killed in Action. Aero Cert 3448, 27 Aug 1916.
			Observer:	Sub Lt R C White-side RNVR Killed in Action.
15.	27 Dec	FE2b	11 Sqn 7666	Crash landed inside Allied lines near Ficheux.
			Pilot:	Lt John Bowley Quested RFC (later Major, MC, C de G,) – unhurt.
			Observer:	Lt H J H Dicksee RFC – wounded.

1917

16.	4 Jan	Sopwith Pup	8 Sqn N5193 RNAS	OP over Bapaume, seen in combat with hostile aircraft.
			Pilot:	Fl Lt Allan Switzer Todd RN Aero Cert 1725, 4 Sept 1915.
17.	23 Jan	FE8	40 Sqn 6388	Line Patrol & Escort near Lens, t/off 1.12 pm, seen to fall in flames.
			Pilot:	2/Lt John Hay RFC, aged 28, Killed in Action. From New

				South Wales, Aero Cert 3039, 2 June '16
18.	24 Jan	FE2b	25 Sqn 6997	Photo Op to Rouvroy, t/off 9.50 am
			Pilot:	Capt Oscar Greig RFC. Prisoner of War & wounded. Aero Cert 1276, 29 May 1916.
			Observer:	Lt J E Maclennan, Cam H'landers att'd RFC. POW & wounded.
19.	1 Feb	BE2d	16 Sqn 6742	Photo Op to Thelus. Forced down inside German lines and destroyed by shell fire 20 minutes later.
			Pilot:	Lt P W Murray, from Durham. Died of Wounds.
			Observer:	Lt T D McRae, Canadian. Died of Wounds.
20.	14 Feb	BE2d	2 Sqn 6231	Art Obs to Lens, t/off 9.45 am, forced down near Loos.
			Pilot:	2/Lt Cyril Douglas Bennett RFC(SR)

				Wounded and Prisoner of War.
				Aged 19, Aero Cert 3189, 4 July '16
			Observer:	2/Lt H A Croft RFC(GL)
21.	14 Feb	BE2d	8 Sqn 6252	T/off 10.35 am, returned after a combat with German scout, with the Observer wounded.
			Pilot:	2/Lt W J Pearson RFC

[There is still a question over this victory. Previously thought to be a Morane of 3 Squadron (Lt T S Green and 2/Lt W K Carse) but they were shot down on the 13th by Jasta 1.]

22.	4 Mar	Sopwith 1½ Strutter	43 Sqn A1108	OP South of Vimy, t/off 1.40 pm. fell to pieces in the air.
			Pilot:	2/Lt H J Green RFC)(SR), aged 19 from Newcastle; Ed at Oxford. Killed in Action.
			Observer:	2/Lt A W Reid MC, 1/6 KOSB & RFC. Killed in Action.
23.	4 Mar	BE2C	2 Sqn 5785	Art Obs.
			Pilot:	Sgt J E Prance (2008) – Wounded in the leg but got home safely.
			Observer:	Lt J B E Crosbee.

[Previously thought to have been a BE of 8 Squadron (F/Sgt R J Moody and 2/Lt E E Horn), but they were shot down by Werner Voss of Jasta 2.]

24.	6 Mar	BE2e	16 Sqn A2785	Art Obs over Vimy, t/off 1.50 pm. Fell over Souchez.
			Pilot:	2/Lt Gerald Maurice Gossett-Bibby RFC (SR); Killed in Action. Born 1897, had been NCO Observer. To France as pilot, Feb 1917.
			Observer:	Lt Geoffrey J A Britchta 2nd Can Mounted Rifles, att'd RFC. Killed in Action.
25.	9 Mar	DH2	29 Sqn A2571	Escort, t/off 9.20 am. Seen to fall in flames over Bailleul.
			Pilot:	Lt A J Pearson MC Royal Fus & RFC. Killed in Action. Fusiliers in 1914, MC March 1915; To France as pilot, December 1916.
26.	11 Mar	BE2d	2 Sqn 6232	Photo Op, t/off 10.30 am, seen to fall over Givenchy.

		Pilot:		2/Lt John Smyth RFC(SR) Killed in Action.
		Observer:		2/Lt Edward Byrne, 4th Gordon Highlanders, att RFC. Aged 37. An old soldier; wounded in France 1915.
27.	17 Mar	FE2b	25 Sqn A5439	Photo escort to Vitry (43 Sqn).
		Pilot:		Lt A E Boultbee, 3rd N'Hants/RFC Killed in Action.
		Observer:		2AM F King (P14996) Killed in Action.
28.	17 Mar	BE2C	16 Sqn 2814	Art Obs over Farbus, t/off 3.25 pm and attacked by enemy scout. Fell inside British lines – wrecked.
		Pilot:		2/Lt George Macdonald Watt RFC Killed in Action. A Scot aged 27; to France Jan 1917.
		Observer:		Sgt F A Howlett Killed in Action.
29.	21 Mar	BE2f	16 Sqn A3154	Art Obs, t/off 3 pm, fell inside British lines near La Neuville.

			Pilot:	F/Sgt Sidney Herbert Quicke (711) Killed in Action. From London. Aero Cert 3890, 27 Nov 1916.
			Observer:	2/Lt W J Lidsey 4/Ox & Bucks LI att'd RFC. Died of Wounds.
30.	24 Mar	SPAD SVII	19 Sqn A6706	OP Lens, fell near Givenchy.
			Pilot:	Lt Richard P Baker RFC Prisoner of War & Wounded.
31.	25 Mar	Nieuport 17	29 Sqn A6689	Escort duty, t/off 7.05 am. Crashed near Tilloy.
			Pilot:	Lt C G Gilbert RFC. Prisoner of War.
32.	2 Apl	BE2d	13 Sqn 5841	Photo Op, t/off 7.47 am, went down over Farbus, crashed into a house.
			Pilot:	Lt Patrick John Gordon Powell ASC & RFC – Killed in Action. Aero Cert 3686, 16 June 1916.

			Observer:	AM P Bonner – Killed in Action.
33. 2 Apl	Sopwith 1½ Strutter	43 Sqn A2401		Photo Op, east of Vimy, t/off at 10.30 am, seen to spin down over Givenchy.
			Pilot:	2/Lt A Peter Warren RFC, aged 19. Prisoner of War.
			Observer:	Sgt R Dunn – Killed in Action. Aged 24 from Newcastle.
34. 3 Apl	FE2b	25 Sqn A6382		Line Patrol Lens-Arras-Bapaume, t/off 8 am – engaged by 8 EA.
			Pilot:	2/Lt Donald P McDonald RFC Prisoner of War.
			Observer:	2/Lt Jack I M O'Bierne 6/Royal Warwick Rgt, att'd RFC. Killed in Action. Aged 23, was wounded in 1915. In 1917 his brother was killed with the RFC.
35. 5 Apl	Bristol F2A	48 Sqn A3340		OP, led by Capt W L Robinson VC,

late morning. Four
Bristols shot down
by Jasta 11.

Pilot: 2/Lt A N Leckler
RFC
Prisoner of War &
Wounded.

Observer: 2/Lt H D K George,
R. Dublin Fus, att'd
RFC, aged 19.
Died of Wounds.
Sandhurst 1914,
France till July
1916, trans RFC
March 1917.

36. 5 Apl   Bristol F2A   48 Sqn A3343   Ditto above –
Pilot: Lt A T Adams,
Wilts Rgt & RFC
Prisoner of War &
wounded.

Observer: Lt D J Stewart,
2/Yorks & Lancs,
Prisoner of War.

37. 7 Apl   Nieuport
17   60 Sqn A6645   Special Op, t/off
4.40 pm.
Pilot: 2/Lt George Orme
Smart RFC
Killed in Action.
Age 19 from
Manchester, former
RFC mechanic.
Commissioned in

				the field for gallantry 1916.
38.	8 Apl	Sopwith 1½ Strutter	43 Sqn A2406	Line Patrol, 1st Army area, t/off 10.30 am seen in combat over Farbus 11.35.
			Pilot:	Lt J S Heagerty, 9/West Kent Rgt & RFC, aged 20. Prisoner of War & wounded. Saw service at Gallipoli.
			Observer:	Lt L Health-Cantle 2/1 Surrey Yeo, Killed in Action, aged 22.
39.	8 Apl	BE2g	16 Sqn A2815	Photo Op to Farbus, t/off 3 pm and seen shot down West of Vimy by EA.
			Pilot:	2/Lt Keith Ingleby MacKenzie, A & S Highlanders & RFC, aged 18. Killed in Action. Aero Cert 2906 17 May 1916.
			Observer:	2/Lt Guy Everingham R. Welch Fus. Killed in Action. France Feb 1915, trans to RFC Sept 1916. Married Feb

1917. Brother killed at Gallipoli.

40. 11 Apl BE2c   13 Sqn 2501   Art Obs, 17th Corps Front, t/off 8.05 am; crashed in front lines, crew wounded but safe.

Pilot: Lt Edward Claude England Derwin RFC
Aero Cert 1484, 29 July 1915.

Observer: Gunner R Pierson.

41. 13 Apl RE8   59 Sqn A3190   Photo Op & Escort to Etaing, t/off 8 am. All six of Squadron's RE's shot down by Jasta 11.

Pilot: Capt James Stewart RFC, Irish from Coleraine, Killed in Action.

Observer: Lt M H Wood, from Essex, Killed in Action.

42. 13 Apl FE2b   11 Sqn A831   OP, t/off 11.25 am, fell inside British lines near Monchy.

Pilot: Sgt James Allen Cunnliffe (11820) Aero Cert 3698, 15 October 1916. Wounded.

	Observer:	2AM W J Batten RFC (46731) Wounded.

43. 13 Apl   FE2b

25 Sqn 4997		Bomb Raid to Henin-Lietard. T/off 6.40 pm, all three FEs shot down on return flight.
	Pilot:	2/Lt Allan Harold Bates, aged 20. Killed in Action. Had been on the Squadron just 10 days.
	Observer:	Sgt William Alfred Barnes (61925) Killed in Action. Was credited with three victories as gunner.

44. 14 Apl   Nieuport
17

60 Sqn A6796		OP east of Douai, t/off 8.30 am. All four aircraft on patrol shot down.
	Pilot:	Lt William Oswald Russell RFC, Prisoner of War Aero Cert 1738, 12 Sept 1915. From London, Russell said his engine hit by two-seater gunner.

45.	16 Apl	BE2C	4 Sqn 5869	Art Obs over Savy, fell inside the British lines near Bailleul, late afternoon.
			Pilot:	Lt Willie Green, Black Watch & RFC Wounded, with fractured skull and broken leg. Age 26, from Scotland.
			Observer:	Lt Cecil Eustace Wilson RFC. Killed in Action, aged 23.
46.	22 Apl	FE2b	11 Sqn 7020	Photo Op, six aircraft, t/off c. 2.30 pm. One fell in German lines four, inc this machine, inside Br lines at Lagnicourt and wrecked.
			Pilot:	Lt W F Fletcher RFC Wounded/injured
			Observer:	Lt W Franklin, Dorset Rgt, att RFC Wounded in leg.
47.	23 Apl	BE2e	4 Sqn A3168	Photo Op East of Vimy, t/off 9.25 am. Down at Mericourt.
			Pilot:	2/Lt E A Welch RFC Killed in Action

			Observer:	Sgt Alfred Tollervey Killed in Action.
48.	28 Apl	BE2e	13 Sqn 7221	Art Obs, 17 Corps Front, t/off 7.20 am. Crashed at Pelves.
			Pilot:	Lt Reginald William Follit RFA/RFC, Died of Wounds. Aged 26 from London, also served in HAC as NCO.
			Observer:	2/Lt F J Kirkham, aged 23. Prisoner of War & wounded.
49.	29 Apl	SPAD SVII	19 Sqn B1573	OP Lens, c.Midday. All three Spads of patrol shot down by Jasta 11.
			Pilot:	Lt R Applin Killed in Action.
50.	29 Apl	FE2b	18 Sqn 4898	Escort, Vth Army area, t/off 2.20 pm; shot down in flames by EA over front lines near Inchy.
			Pilot:	Sgt G Stead, aged 19 from Manchester Killed in Action – had been in France just 8 days.

			Observer:	Cpl Alfred Beebee Killed in Action.
51.	29 Apl	BE2e	12 Sqn 2738	Art Obs, t/off 4.45 pm, crashed at Roeux near front lines.
			Pilot:	Lt D E Davies, Killed in Action.
			Observer:	Lt G H Rathbone, Killed in Action.
52.	29 Apl	Nieuport 17	40 Sqn A6745	OP, fell near Billy-Montigny early evening.
			Pilot:	Capt Frederick Leycester Barwell Killed in Action.
53.	18 Jun	RE8	9 Sqn A4290	Photo Op, t/off 11 am.
			Pilot:	Lt R W Ellis – Killed in Action.
			Observer:	Lt H C Barlow – Killed in Action.
54.	23 Jun	SPAD		Shot down evening, north of Ypres: no RFC losses recorded – possibly Belgian or French machine.
55.	24 Jun	DH4	57 Sqn A7473	Photo Op to Bacelaere – 0930 am.

	Pilot:	Capt Norman George Mc-Naughton MC, Aero Cert 1453, 21 July 1915.
	Observer:	Lt A H Mearns.

[Past confusion over this victory due to times. McNaughton took off at 7.40 am and was shot down at 9.30 am, and not 9.30 pm!]

56. 25 Jun	RE8	53 Sqn A3847	Art Obs, t/off pm, shot down into front lines at 4.35 pm – wrecked.
		Pilot:	Lt Leslie Spencer Bowman 4th Kings Owns R.Lancs Rgt & RFC, aged 20. Killed in Action.
		Observer:	2/Lt J E Power-Clutterbuck RFA att RFC, aged 23. Killed in Action. Only son of Surgeon Major E R Power AMS.

57. 2 Jul	RE8	53 Sqn A3538	Escort to Photo Op, shot down in flames behind Comines at 8.40 am.
		Pilot:	Sgt Herbert Arthur Whatley RFC Killed in Action. Aero Cert 4515, 16 April 1917.

			Observer:	2/Lt F G B Pascoe Killed in Action.
58.	16 Aug	Nieuport 23	29 Sqn A6611	OP, t/off 6.25 am, last seen east of Zonnebeke with 8 EA.
			Pilot:	2/Lt W H T Williams RFC(GL)
59.	26 Aug	SPAD SVII	19 Sqn B3492	Escort, t/off 5.18 am.
			Pilot:	2/Lt C P Williams RFC(GL) Killed in Action.
60.	2 Sep	RE8	6 Sqn B782	Art Obs Polygon Wood, t/off 5.50 am, seen shot down by EA.
			Pilot:	Lt J B C Madge RFC(GL)), Prisoner of War & Wounded.
			Observer:	2/Lt W Kember.
61.	3 Sep	Sopwith Pup	46 Sqn B1795 Pilot:	OP, t/off 7.35 am. Lt A F Bird, Norfolk Rgt & RFC Prisoner of War.
62.	23 Nov	DH5	64 Sqn A9299	Ground strafe, Bourlon Wood, t/off 12.40 pm.
			Pilot:	Lt James A V Boddy Wounded but

rescued from front
lines with two bro-
ken thighs.

63. 30 Nov	SE5a	41 Sqn B644	OP to Moevres, t/off 1 pm and shot down in flames.
		Pilot:	Lt D A D I Macgregor

[Previously thought to be Capt R T Townsend of 56 Squadron, but he went down to Josef Mai of Jasta 5.]

1918

64. 12 Mar	Bristol F2B	62 Sqn B1251	OP, t/off 9.30 am, fell in flames E of Cambrai about 11.10 am
		Pilot:	2/Lt L C F Clutterbuck RFC(GL) Prisoner of War.
		Observer:	2/Lt H J Sparks MC, KRRC att'd RFC Prisoner of War & wounded.

65. 13 Mar	Sopwith Camel	73 Sqn B5590	Op, t/off 9.35 am. Went down over Gonnelieu, SE of Cambrai.
		Pilot:	2/Lt J M L Millett, Canadian. Killed in Action.

66. 18 Mar   Sopwith
                Camel   54 Sqn B5243   OP Busigny, t/off 10 am, last seen in fight with EA. The patrol lost five Camels.

                               Pilot: 2/Lt William G Ivamy, Canadian Prisoner of War.

67. 24 Mar   SE5a   41 Sqn   OP to Havrincourt, t/off 2.10 pm.

                               Pilot: Either Lt J P McCone in C1054, or 2/Lt D C Tucker in C6399.

[Previously identified as 2/Lt W Porter, 56 Squadron. 41 Sqn were in combat with Fokker Triplanes in the Sailly-Havrincourt area at around 3 pm German time, Porter went down earlier near Peronne.]

68. 25 Mar   Sopwith
                Camel   3 Sqn C1562   Low bombing, 3rd Army front, t/off 3.30 pm – fell in flames.

                               Pilot: 2/Lt Donald Cameron RFC(GL)
Killed in Action

69. 26 Mar   Sopwith
                Camel   54 Sqn C1568   OP, t/off 12.45 pm, last seen near Roye – crashed at Contalmaison.
2/Lt A T W Lindsay

70.	26 Mar	RE8	15 Sqn B742	Patrol & bombing in Corps area, t/off 4.10 pm. Crashed Albert.
			Pilot:	2/Lt A V Reading – Killed in Action
			Observer:	2/Lt Matt Leggat – Killed in Action
71.	27 Mar	Sopwith Camel	70 Sqn C8234	Low flying patrol, Albert area, t/off 9 am, fell near Aveluy.
			Pilot:	Lt H W Ransom, aged 21. Killed in Action. Had served in South Africa.
72.	27 Mar	Bristol F2B	20 Sqn B1156	Low bombing, Albert area – pm.
			Pilot:	Capt K R Kirkham MC – POW
			Observer:	Capt J H Hedley CdG – POW

[There is stronger evidence that Richthofen did not bring down Kirkham and Hedley but possibly a DH4 of 5 Naval Squadron, which lost D8379 during a raid on Foucaucourt (where Richthofen claimed his victim fell) – FSL E C Stocker & AGL C M Rendle, or perhaps even a AWKF8 of 2 Sqn – B288 with Lt E T Smart/2/Lt K P Barford. It was a very confused afternoon in the battle area during the March push, but 5 Naval did have a fight with Triplanes. Richthofen claimed his victim went down on fire which the Bristol clearly did not.]

73. 27 Mar   Sopwith   79 Sqn C4016   OP, t/off 3.30 pm
             Dolphin   Pilot: ̄   2/Lt G H Harding

[Originally thought to be a Bristol F2B (B1332) flown by Capt H R Child, of 11 Sqn but Richthofen said there was no gunner and the rear cockpit was covered over. But Child did have an observer, Lt A Reeve. It is believed that Richthofen, who probably hadn't seen a Dolphin before, thought, with its twin wing bays, that the Dolphin was a Bristol. It is also possible that it could have been a Dolphin of 19 Sqn – 2/Lt E J Blyth, C3790.]

74. 28 Mar   AWFK8   82 Sqn C8444   Recce   Op – pm, crashed near Mericourt early afternoon.
                                    Pilot: 2/Lt J B Taylor – Killed in Action
                                    Observer: 2/Lt E Betley – Killed in Action

75. 2 Apl   RE8   52 Sqn A3868   Bombing patrol, front lines. T/off 12 noon, crashed at Moreuil.
                                      Pilot: 2/Lt E D Jones – Killed in Action
                                    Observer: 2/Lt R F Newton – Killed in Action

76. 6 Apl   Sopwith Camel   46 Sqn D6491   Low bombing 3rd Army front, t/off 2.45 pm, went down over Villers-Bretonneux at 3.30 pm.

	Pilot:	Capt Sydney Philip Smith ASC & RFC. Killed in Action, aged 22 from Surrey. Previously with 6 Sqn and wounded 1 May 1917. Aero Cert No. 3056, 24 May 1916.

77. 7 Apl	Sopwith Camel	73 Sqn D6550	OP near Lamotte, t/off 10.10 am, force landed after fight with EA, W of Villers Bretonneux – safe.
	Pilot:		2/Lt A V Gallie.

[This victory has often been said to be over Capt G B Moore of 1 Sqn, but the location is way off, and eye witnesses in the patrol reported he was hit by an AA shell and disintegrated. Moore was also flying an SE5a! There is also a suggestion that the victim was another SE5a pilot – Lt P J Nolan DFC of 24 Sqn but he was shot down in mid-afternoon.]

78. 7 Apl	SPAD	No RFC losses, possibly a French machine, as French units were in the area at this time.

[It is possible that in fact this was another Camel of 73 Squadron, who lost two Camels in this fight with two more badly shot up. Richthofen didn't actually see this second victory crash, so it could have been either of the two damaged Camels, flown by Capt M LeBlanc-Smith (D1839) or Lt A N Baker in (D1823). Lt R G H Adams (D6554) was the other loss, believed shot down by Hans Kirschstein with Ltn Wolff claiming another as forced to land. (Adams later became the famous actor Ronald Adam, and a fighter controller in WW2.)]

79. 20 Apl	Sopwith Camel	3 Sqn D6439	OP, 3rd Army front, t/off 5.30 pm, Crashed Bois de Hamel.
	Pilot:		Major Richard Raymond-Barker MC, 12th Nth'land Fus & RFC Killed in Action. Aero Cert 1460 18 July, 1915.
80. 20 Apl	Sopwith Camel	3 Sqn B7390	OP, 3rd Army front, t/off 5.30 pm, crashed Villers-Bretonneux.
	Pilot:		2/Lt D G Lewis, Rhodesian, age 19. Prisoner of War.

Appendix 2
AIRCRAFT FLOWN BY MANFRED von RICHTHOFEN

by N.H. Hauprich

Note	Vict.	Type	Serial	Jasta	Remarks
1.	1–17	Alb DII	D491/17	2	Red added after 14th vict, locations UKN.
	18	Alb DIII	D789/17	11	Cracked spar, top wing, after this vict.
2.	19–24	Halb DII		11	
	25	Alb DIII		11	This was Lübbert's A/C.
	26–31	Halb DII			
3.	32–52	Alb DIII	D2253/17	11	Also possibly flew Alb DIII D789/17. D2253/17 was red as follows: spinner, fuse, hor tail, rudder, fin, struts. Fuse & fin Cross Patee overpainted but black crosses show up faintly. Albatros logo on rudder not overpainted. Sometime after March 1917 the fuse cross was crudely repainted in white outline. Std mauve/dark green upper wing surfaces, turquoise undersurfaces.
	53	Alb DIII	D789/17	11	Red, no other data available.
	54–57	Alb DV	D1177/17	11	Red: Fuse, vert tail, wheel covers, struts,

No.	Type	Serial	Unit	Notes
				spinner. Wings, hor tail-std mauve/dark green upper surfaces, turquoise undersurfaces. All Patee Crosses outlined in white. JG 1 was formed on June 26, 1917.
58–59	Alb DV	D2059/17	11 JG 1	Red: fuse, hor tail, wheel covers, spinner, all struts. Rudder lozenge fabric, fin natural varnish. Wings std mauve/dark green upper surfaces, turquoise undersurfaces. Fuse cross had white borders overpainted.
60–61	Fok FI	102/17	11 JG 1	Std Fokker streaked finish, natural aluminium cowl. Patee Crosses on white field, white rudder. Turquoise undersurfaces on wings, hor tail, fuse. Fokker Werke Nr. 1729. Tested on Aug. 16, 1917. Delivered on Aug, 21, 1917. Obltn. Kurt Wolff KIA in this A/C on Sept. 15, 1917 by McGregor of Naval 10.
62–63	Alb DVa	D4693/17	11 JG 1	Red engine hood, tail. Aircraft sent to Berlin Museum.

Note	Vict.	Type	Serial	Jasta	Remarks
	64–66	Fok DR.I	152/17	11 JG 1	Red cowl, wheel covers, rear aft fuse from fwd edge of cross, struts, top surface of upper wing, rudder with white border on crosses. Balance of A/C std Fokker factory finish.
		Fok DR.I	152/17		Fokker Werke Nr. 1864 Tested on Nov, 2, 1917 Delivered on Dec 13, 1917 Returned to Fokker works, Schwerin, on Mar 18, 1918 for wing modification.
	67–70	Fok DR.I	477/17	11 JG 1	Original markings: Red upper hood, deck, wheel covers, tail unit. A/C recovered in silk, painted all red with Cross Patee outlined in white after 75th V. Fokker Werke Nr. 2103
5.	71,74, 76–78	Fok DR.I	127/17	11 JG 1	Red cowling, wheel covers, hood(?), tail. This from combat report but photos show hor tail is streaked factory finish. Rudder had a streaked finish and Cross Patee with white border. Patee Crosses on wings & fuse on white fields.

186

Balance of A/C in std factory finish.
Fokker Werke Nr. 1838
Tested on Oct 15, 1917
Delivered on Oct 29, 1917
See above, victories 76 to 70

Red sides & top deck of fuse, upper surfaces of all wings, all struts, wheel covers, hor tail. White rudder. All Patee Crosses over-painted to broad style Balkan crosses, Patee Crosses show thru on fuse locations and upper wing locations. Turquoise under-surfaces on fuse & wings.
Engine: Oberursel 110 HP, serial 2478. These engines were almost direct copies of the Le Rhone and sometimes identified as such.
Fokker Werke Nr. 2009
Tested on Jan 8, 1918 by Weidner.

	72,73,75	Fok DR.I	477/17	11 / JG 1
6.	79,80	Fok DR.I	425/17	11 / JG 1

Note	Vict.	Type	Serial	Jasta	Remarks
The following aircraft were also flown by M.v.R. but he had no victories with them;					
		Alb DV	1033/17		. . red spinner, nose band, hor & vert tail, top surface of upper wing. Fin & rudder crosses and on top wing were overpainted, black shows thru very faintly. Black (?) narrow band around fuse at fwd edge of hor tail. Balance of A/C in std factory finish. Suffered head wound while flying this A/C on July 2, 1917.
		Fok. DR.I	114/17		. . crashed on Oct 30, 1917 in emergency landing to help Lothar. A/C not rebuilt.
		Fok DR.I	119/17		. . damaged in forced landing.

Notes:

1. There are questions as to whether this was 481/17 or 491/17, but believed to be 491.
2. "von Richthofen and the 'Flying Circus'", Harleyford, page 44–45 states that M.v.R. again flew an Alb D III in April 1917 scoring victory 32. This would indicate that he flew the Halberstadt DII for victories 19 to 31 inclusive.
3. Some sources indicate this A/C was serial D2253/17 but this is probably too high a serial for this period of time.
4. Both Fl 102/17 and Fl 103/17 (W. Voss) had curved leading edges to the hor stabilizer. Also, there was no painted thrust line or weight table.

5. There is some controversy concerning this A/C. Records exist indicating M.v.R. obtained victories 71, 74, 76, 77 and 78 in this A/C. Photos of this A/C with Ltn. Koch and Ltn. Hunolstein show this triplane in std factory finish with white rudder. M.v.R.'s 127/17 had an overpainted rudder. Was the rudder replaced or repainted? 127/17 was transfered to Jasta 32 later. Is it possible that 127/17 belonged to another Jasta 11 pilot and used by M.v.R. as a standby?

6. Some sources indicate that 425/17 was "all red". The photo in the Harleyford book on page 85 shows that all the triplanes in the lineup had a lighter tone to the undersides of the wings. This photo was taken after the conversion to the Balkan cross. In my correspondence with the late Gen. der Flieger Karl Bodenschatz he stated that M.v.R. never flew an "all red" triplane in combat.

References:

1. von Richthofen and the "Flying Circus", Harleyford, 2nd ed, 1959.
2. Jagd in Flanderns Himmel, Karl Bodenschatz
3. Red Knight of Germany, Gibbons.
4. Richthofen, The Red Knight of the Air, Vigilant
5. The Red Air Fighter, M.v.Richthofen.
6. Richthofen, von Italiaander
7. Eagles of the Black Cross, Musciano
8. Fokker Fighters of World War I, Grey & Stair
9. Richthofen's Dreidecker and Fokker D VII, Nowarra.
10. Cross & Cockade Journals (U.S.A.)
11. Air Enthusiast, No. 8

189

Appendix 3
Notes

by N.H. Hauprich

p. 35: Bölcke: Although in English the German umlaut is frequently replaced by an 'e' following the vowel, in the case of Oswald Boelcke he himself was accustomed to spelling it with the 'e', although the rest of his family used the umlaut, as does the editor to the first edition in English, C.G. Grey.

p. 63: 69th Squadron: Feldfliegerabteilung Nr 69.

p. 71: Editor's footnote: Not a Gotha but either an AEG G–I or G–II. Both were 3-place aircraft with tractor propellers.

p. 79: Second Fighting Squadron: Kampfgeschwader Nr 2.

p. 80: Upwards firing gun: This may have been a captured Lewis gun, as a Parabellum 7.92 mm gun, in spite of its light weight of 22 lb, would have been a little bulky due to the ammunition drum.

p. 89: Editor's footnote: It is now known that both sides made use of aircraft in attacking ground targets, for example the British at Cambrai, and in the last year of the war.

p. 96: Death of Boelcke: Boelcke collided with Ltn Erwin Boehme who later became CO of Jasta 2 from 28th August 1917

190

to 29th November, 1917, when he was killed near Zonnebeke after gaining 24 victories.

p. 98: Ltn Imelmann: Correct identification is Ltn Hans Imelmann (note spelling). Flew with Jasta 2 from Oct 1916 to 24th January 1917 when he was killed through a wing failure of his Albatros DIII south of Miramont. Born on 14th May, 1897, in Hannover, he had six victories. He was no relation to Max Immelmann.

p. 98: Eighth victory: details will be found in Appendix 1. Although Richtholen mentions that he wounded the gunner, the pilot, 2nd Lt J.G. Cameron, was flying alone, obviously in order to carry an extra bomb load.

p. 112: Ltn Lübbert: Correct spelling is Lübbert/Luebbert. Ltn Eduard Lübbert, born 29th December 1893 in Hamburg, killed in action on 30th March 1917 at Bailleul.

p. 113: There is still controversy concerning the fight in which Werner Voss was killed. It is possible that Lt Rhys-Davids did not shoot Voss down.

p. 118: Schäfer: Ltn Emil Schäfer, born 17th December, 1891 in Krefeld-Bockum, joined Jasta 11 soon after Manfred von Richthofen took command. He took command of Jasta 28 from 27th April, 1917, but was killed in action on 5th June, 1917, after 30 victories.

p. 119: Wolff: Ltn Kurt Wolff, born on 6th February, 1895 in Griefswald, transferred to Jasta 11 from Jasta 29 in June 1917. Wounded in action on 11th July, 1917, he returned to Jasta 11 on 11th September and was killed near Nachtigal while flying von Richthofen's Fokker FI 102/17, on 15th September, after 33 victories.

Manfred von Richthofen is credited with only two, not three as he states, victories on 2nd April 1917.

p. 135: Wedel: There were two Wedel brothers, Obltn Ernst Rüdiger von Wedel, who flew with Jasta 11 till the end of the war (acting CO from 26.7.18 to 14.8.18, 31.8.18 to 2.9.18, 4.9.18 to 22.10.18 and 4.11.18 to EOW), gaining 13 victories, and Obltn Hasso von Wedel who served as CO of Jasta 75 in 1918.

p. 136: 'fat two-seater': A DFW CV. Ltn Krefft joined Jasta 11 in November 1916 and later became the Technical Officer of JG Nr 1 (Richthofen).

p. 148: Albert Ball: It has never been explained why Lothar von Richthofen claimed a triplane when Ball was flying an SE5 when he was killed on 7th May, 1917. They did have a fight on 7th May 1917, but it is in doubt whether Lothar actually shot him down.

The date of Lothar being wounded, 5th May, should read 7th May – after the Ball fight when he was hit by ground fire.